BIRDS

WARD LOCK

A KINGFISHER BOOK
First published in Great Britain in 1978
by Ward Lock Limited, 116 Baker Street, London, W1M 2BB,
a Pentos company

Reprinted 1979 (twice), 1980

Designed and produced by Grisewood & Dempsey Ltd
Grosvenor House, 141-143 Drury Lane, London WC2
© Grisewood & Dempsey Ltd 1978
All Rights Reserved

Colour separations by Newsele Litho Ltd, Milan, London
Printed and bound by Vallardi Industrie Grafiche, Milan

BRITISH LIBRARY CATALOGUING IN PUBLICATION DATA
Ardley, Neil
  Birds.—(Kingfisher guides).
  1. Birds—Europe—Juvenile literature
  I. Title   II. Series
  598.2'94   QL690

  ISBN 0-7063-5446-X

The Publishers wish to thank the following for their kind help in
supplying photographs for this book:

*Bruce Coleman, cover, pages 57 & 83. Brian Hawkes, pages 12,
14, 18, 22, 26, 32, 41, 51, 62, 65, 67, 75, 79, 80, 82, 85, 86, 90, 97,
102, 106, 117, 119. Eric & David Hosking, pages 48 & 113. NHPA,
title page Dalton, page 47 Joe Blossom, page 110 E. A. Jones.
ZEFA, 6, 7. Picture research: Penny Warn.*

AUTHOR
NEIL ARDLEY

ILLUSTRATOR
MARTIN CAMM

EDITOR
ERIC INGLEFIELD

ASSISTANT EDITOR
POH CHEEN HORN

CONSULTANT ORNITHOLOGISTS
PETER OLNEY
Curator of Birds
Zoological Society of London

BRIAN HAWKES

INTRODUCTION

Naming Birds

Several different features can help you to identify a bird. Its shape, size and pattern of colours are usually enough to be sure of its name, but some birds look rather alike. In these cases, it may help to know the kind of countryside in which the bird is found and in which countries it lives. The way in which it moves and flies and the kind of song that it sings may also help to name a bird.

In this guide, the birds are placed in groups called *orders* or *families*. Each group has a short introduction that gives its Latin name, and describes the general features of the birds in each group and any interesting points about them as a group. On the same page are full-colour paintings of each bird in the group. The paintings show any differences between the male and female, and any changes in colour that occur in different seasons of the year. If the caption to the painting does not say that the bird is a male or female, then the male and female look alike and cannot be told apart. On some pages there are also colour photographs that show some of the birds in characteristic activities. In the text accompanying each painting is a description of each bird giving its usual English name, its Latin or scientific name (genus and species), its size from the tip of its beak to the end of its tail in centimetres (cm) and inches (in), and a description of its habits and the kind of places in which it is likely to be seen. Any special points of interest are added.

Identifying Birds

As well as several paintings and descriptions of birds, each two-page spread also has a table called *What To Look For* and a set of maps. These will be very helpful in naming birds. The table gives the features that must be seen to be sure of a bird's identity. These are the features that birdwatchers look for. For example, to identify a great tit (pages 90–91), you need only look for a yellow breast with a black central stripe. The various parts of a bird mentioned in the tables are shown in the illustration of a male chaffinch on the opposite page.

Each map shows in which parts of Europe a bird is to be found. In a purple area, the bird may be seen all the year round. In a blue area, it will be found only from late autumn through the winter to early spring. In a pink area, it will be seen only from late spring through summer to early autumn. In a white area, it is not likely to be found at any time, unless migrating between a pink and blue area in spring or autumn.

Bird songs are not described in this book, except in the case of warblers (pages 100–107); recognizing a song may be the only way to identify

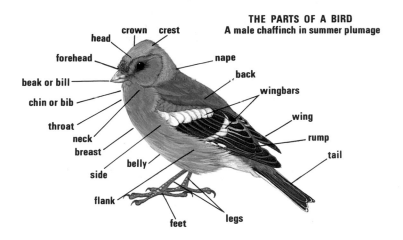

THE PARTS OF A BIRD
A male chaffinch in summer plumage

crown crest

head

forehead

beak or bill

chin or bib

throat

neck

breast

belly

side

flank

feet

legs

nape

back

wingbars

wing

rump

tail

these birds. It is difficult to describe a song in words, and the best way to learn bird song is from an experienced birdwatcher or from records.

With this guide, you should be able to name any bird that you are likely to see anywhere in Europe. It contains 353 kinds of birds, consisting of all those that live in this region except for a few very rare birds and some that live only on the edge of Europe. However, birds may sometimes be seen in other places than those mentioned and possibly in other countries than those shown on the maps. Some birds may also look slightly different from their paintings, especially if the light is dim.

The Names of Birds

In the classification of birds, each different kind of bird usually belongs to a separate species and is identified by two Latin names, a *genus* name followed by a *species* name. Similar species of birds belong to the same genus – for example, all the European divers are similar species in the genus *Gavia*. Sometimes three Latin names are given – see the wagtails (pages 112–113) for example. In these cases, the bird is a *subspecies* and belongs to the same species as another subspecies. The two subspecies look slightly different and live in different places, but they may interbreed where they meet. Birds in similar genera (the plural of genus) are grouped together in the same family, and similar families are grouped together in the same order.

This book follows the sequence of orders and families recommended by the British Trust for Ornithology. By grouping birds in this way, similar birds are placed close together, making identification easier. An index of English names at the end of the book will help in looking up a particular bird.

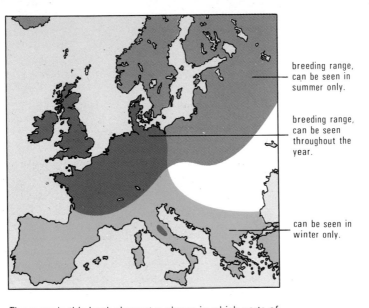

breeding range, can be seen in summer only.

breeding range, can be seen throughout the year.

can be seen in winter only.

The maps in this book show at a glance in which parts of Europe a bird is likely to be found at different times of the year. The pink area indicates the summer range, and blue the winter range. Purple indicates the area where the bird can be seen throughout the year.

Where and When to See Birds

You can see birds almost anywhere at any time, but different kinds of birds live in different places and the same place may have different kinds of birds at different times of the year. It is interesting to study the features that enable a bird to live in a particular place. For example, woodland birds have very different kinds of feet and beaks from sea birds, because they follow very different ways of life. Few birds can easily live in a wide range of places. However, birds of prey, although mainly scarce nowadays, are to be seen at most kinds of coast and countryside and even in towns.

Some places have greater numbers of birds than others. Every country has natural meeting places for birds where they often gather in huge flocks. Many of these have been made into bird reserves, where the birds are protected so that they can live and nest in safety. At these places, there are often facilities to help birdwatchers to see the birds easily.

The Start of the Bird's Year

A bird's year begins in the early spring, when it prepares to build a nest, lay eggs and raise its young. At this time it begins to behave differently. Some birds migrate – they fly north to particular places known as breeding grounds where they will find enough food to feed their young. Many sea birds come to the shore to nest after roaming the ocean during the winter, while several shore birds fly inland to raise their young. Other birds find enough food where they are and so do not migrate. But it is during migration that unusual birds are most likely to be seen, for the birds take time to reach their breeding grounds. They may stop here and there on the way and be blown off course.

The Breeding Season

As the breeding season approaches, many birds become more brightly coloured or even change part of their plumage completely. This helps the male and female birds to identify each other, but they may also attract one another by singing and making strange postures or dances. Fighting may also occur between rival birds. As the birds form pairs, they may build nests for their eggs. However, many birds lay their eggs on the ground among grass or pebbles or use burrows, hollow trees or holes or ledges in rocks and cliffs to raise their young. By early summer, the first eggs have hatched and the parent birds are busy finding food for their young. Later, the parents may be seen leading their young in search of food.

Moulting and Migration

As summer goes on, many birds seem to disappear. Having raised their young, they *moult*, or change their feathers. A bird is in danger at this time, and so it hides away. The new plumage may have a different pattern, giving the bird its winter dress. As autumn arrives, the birds that arrived in the spring to breed make another great journey south to the lands where they spend the winter. Many of them are insect eaters and have to migrate to the tropics to find food. At the same time, birds that have their breeding grounds in the far north arrive to escape the severe winters there. Birds that have raised their young inland may go to the coast for the winter. Many sea birds leave to spend the winter at sea, while some go inland in search of food. During the winter, the visiting and resident birds may often be seen roaming in flocks among trees and bushes and over open ground in search of food.

Then spring comes and the winter visitors depart for their breeding grounds as the summer visitors arrive and the year begins again.

Studying Birds

Looking at birds wherever you happen to find them is an easy way to begin studying them. However, the amount that you will learn about birds will be limited. Few birds will let you approach them, and if you want to spot particular species or observe certain kinds of behaviour, then you will have to search for them. Joining a bird society or club will help you greatly.

A pair of binoculars is an essential aid. Their power should be from 7×30 to 10×50. Buy the best you can afford but do not get big and heavy binoculars – they are tiring to carry and difficult to hold still. Use binoculars to find birds; by the time you have spotted a bird with the naked eye, raised the binoculars, got the bird in your field of view and focused the binoculars, it will probably have flown away. Be patient and quiet at all times, and wear dark clothes. For close views of birds, you will need to conceal yourself and wait, possibly in a hide, which may be a tent with flaps for windows or perhaps a handy shed.

Always take a notebook and write down your observations. Make notes of the place, date, time, weather, the kind of countryside or coastline, the birds you see and their behaviour, making drawings if necessary. Taking photographs of birds is not easy, but well worth the effort. A telephoto lens will be needed and the best photographs can only be taken from a hide. Electronic flash helps to freeze any action and get sharp close-ups. Recordings of bird song can be made on portable tape or cassette recorders. Placing a parabolic (bowl-shaped) sound reflector around the microphone will improve the quality.

DIVERS

Order Gaviiformes Family Gaviidae

Divers are really at home underwater, where they catch fish and crustaceans. They either dive suddenly from the surface or sink slowly into the water. On land, divers walk clumsily and they normally come ashore only to breed. In winter, all divers become grey-brown above and white below. They can then only be told apart by their size, bill shape and the colours of their backs.

summer

winter

Black-throated Diver

winter

summer

Great Northern Diver

Black-throated Diver

Great Northern Diver

Red-throated Diver

Black-throated Diver *Gavia arctica* 63 cm 25 in. Breeds at remote lakes or lochs, usually on rocky islands. Seen at coasts in autumn and winter, often in small flocks.

Great Northern Diver *Gavia immer* 76 cm 30 in. Breeds on lakes in Iceland. Found at coast at other times.

Red-throated Diver *Gavia stellata* 56 cm 22 in. Breeds at coast and lakes, flying daily to the sea to feed. May be seen on reservoirs and lakes as well as at coast during autumn and winter.

Red-throated Diver

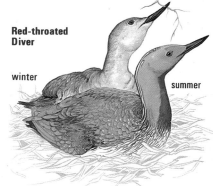

winter

summer

WHAT TO LOOK FOR

Black-throated Diver Thin bill. Summer: black throat patch; dark spotted back. Winter: blackish back.

Great Northern Diver Heavy bill. Summer: all-black head; chequered back. Winter: grey-brown back.

Red-throated Diver Thin upturned bill. Summer: red throat patch; plain grey back. Winter: grey-brown back speckled with white.

13

GREBES

Order Podicipediformes Family Podicipitidae

Grebes are elegant water birds with colourful breeding plumage in spring and summer. The boldly patterned heads and necks, with their ear tufts and frills, clearly mark them out from other birds. In winter, grebes lose their colour and adornments, becoming grey-brown above and white below. Then they look like divers, but are smaller and have wedge-shaped heads.

Grebes feed by diving for fish and other water animals. Although agile in the water, they are not good fliers and may escape danger by partly submerging themselves until only the head remains above water.

Grebes build nests of water plants among reeds at the edges of lakes and rivers, and lay about four eggs. The eggs may be covered with vegetation. Before building the nest, the birds perform extraordinary courtship dances in which they rush to and fro over the water and freeze in absurd postures. The chicks are often carried on the parents' backs, even during dives.

Grebes spread to the coast and open water in autumn and winter. Reservoirs are a good place to see them at this time.

A pair of red-necked grebes in summer plumage. The nest floats among reeds at the edge of a lake. A chick nestles between the wings of the parent bird on the nest.

winter

summer

Little Grebe

Slavonian Grebe

winter

summer

14

Great Crested Grebe *Podiceps cristatus* 46 cm 18 in. Found on inland waters in summer and winter; also at coast in winter. Once hunted for its plumage, it came near to extinction in Britain in 1800s. Recovery mainly due to protection, though building of reservoirs has enabled it to expand.

Red–necked Grebe *Podiceps grisgena* 43 cm 17 in. Found on inland waters in summer; usually at coast in winter.

Slavonian Grebe or **Horned Grebe** *Podiceps auritus* 36 cm 14 in. Found on inland waters in summer and at estuaries in winter.

Black–necked Grebe *Podiceps nigricollis* 30 cm 12 in. Often seen in small flocks on inland waters in summer and at estuaries and inland in winter.

Little Grebe or **Dabchick** *Tachybaptus ruficollis* 25 cm 10 in. Found on inland waters in summer and winter; also at coast in winter.

Great Crested Grebe

Red-necked Grebe

Black-necked Grebe

WHAT TO LOOK FOR

Great Crested Grebe Long white neck and pink bill. Summer: large ear tufts and frill.

Red-necked Grebe Medium-sized neck and black and yellow bill. Summer: red neck and pale grey cheeks but no frill.

Slavonian Grebe Blue-grey bill. Summer: golden ear tufts and chestnut neck. Winter: white cheeks.

Black-necked Grebe Slightly upturned bill. Summer: black neck and chestnut ear tufts. Winter: dusky neck and cheeks.

Little Grebe Duck-like shape with almost no tail. Summer: rust-coloured neck.

Great Crested Grebe

Red-necked Grebe

Slavonian Grebe

Black-necked Grebe

Little Grebe

FULMARS, SHEARWATERS AND PETRELS

Order Procellariiformes

The fulmar and shearwaters (family Procellariidae) and petrels (family Hydrobatidae) are all ocean birds that normally come ashore only to breed. They may then be seen in colonies on coastal cliffs and islands. Some shearwaters are southern birds that visit European waters when migrating. Several species may also be seen following ships. The fulmar and shearwaters are the size of large gulls, but can be told from gulls by the way they glide low over the sea with straight, stiff wings. Shearwaters have narrower wings and thinner, longer bills than the fulmar. Petrels are the smallest European sea birds. They are dark with conspicuous white rumps, and they flutter over the waves.

light phase

Fulmar

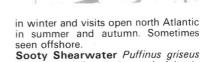

dark phase

Fulmar

Cory's Shearwater

Manx Shearwater

Fulmar *Fulmarus glacialis* 46 cm 18 in. Often follows ships, but may come ashore and occupy buildings. Nests in colonies on cliffs. Parents protect the young by ejecting a foul-smelling oily liquid at intruders. There are two colour phases.

Cory's Shearwater *Calonectris diomedea* 46 cm 18 in. Breeds on Mediterranean islands and ventures into Atlantic in autumn. Does not follow ships.

Manx Shearwater *Puffinus puffinus* 36 cm 14 in. Breeds in colonies in burrows on islands and cliff-tops. Does not follow ships. Commonest European shearwater.

Great Shearwater *Puffinus gravis* 46 cm 18 in. Breeds in south Atlantic in winter and visits open north Atlantic in summer and autumn. Sometimes seen offshore.

Sooty Shearwater *Puffinus griseus* 41 cm 16 in. Breeds in south Atlantic in winter and visits north Atlantic in summer and autumn. May be seen offshore.

Storm Petrel *Hydrobates pelagicus* 15 cm 6 in. Nests in crevices in rocks or stone walls on islands. Can be seen following ships, flitting over the waves summer and autumn. May be seen offshore.

Leach's Petrel *Oceanodroma leucorhoa* 20 cm 8 in. Breeds in burrows on islands. Flight is more erratic than storm petrel, and does not follow ships or patter over waves.

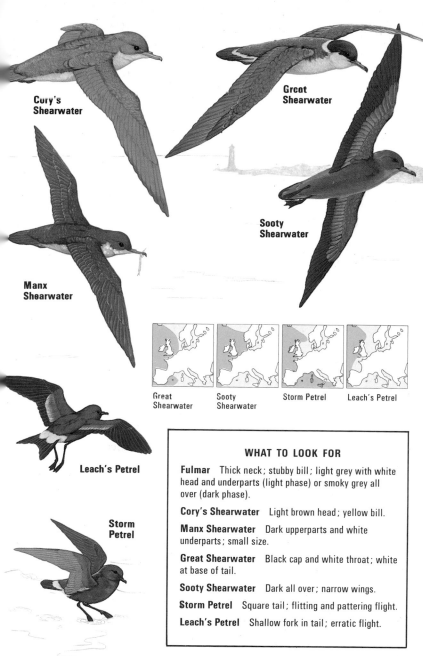

Cory's Shearwater

Great Shearwater

Sooty Shearwater

Manx Shearwater

Leach's Petrel

Storm Petrel

Great Shearwater

Sooty Shearwater

Storm Petrel

Leach's Petrel

WHAT TO LOOK FOR

Fulmar Thick neck; stubby bill; light grey with white head and underparts (light phase) or smoky grey all over (dark phase).

Cory's Shearwater Light brown head; yellow bill.

Manx Shearwater Dark upperparts and white underparts; small size.

Great Shearwater Black cap and white throat; white at base of tail.

Sooty Shearwater Dark all over; narrow wings.

Storm Petrel Square tail; flitting and pattering flight.

Leach's Petrel Shallow fork in tail; erratic flight.

GANNETS, PELICANS AND CORMORANTS

Order Pelecaniformes

A colony of gannets. The young birds are dark in colour.

Gannets (family Sulidae), pelicans (family Pelecanidae) and cormorants (family Phalacrocoracidae) are the largest European sea birds. Although they all have webbed feet, they are not habitual swimmers. They all have different and interesting methods of fishing.

WHAT TO LOOK FOR

Gannet White body with pointed tail; black wingtips; yellow head with blue eye-ring.

White Pelican Underside of wings white at front, dark at rear; flesh-coloured feet.

Dalmatian Pelican Underside of wings all white except for dark wingtips; grey feet.

Cormorant Atlantic form: all black with white chin. Continental form: black with white head and neck.

Shag Green-black; yellow base of bill.

Pygmy Cormorant Breeding: dark spotted plumage; rust-coloured head. Non-breeding: unspotted plumage, white throat, rust-coloured breast.

Gannet *Sula bassana* 91 cm 36 in. Breeds in summer in vast colonies on cliffs of rocky islands. Winters at sea, but may be seen offshore. May follow ships. Makes spectacular dive into the water to catch fish.

White Pelican *Pelecanus onocrotalus* 168 cm 65 in. Breeds in swamps and marshes in eastern Mediterranean. May also be seen at coast in winter. Uses pouch beneath bill as net to catch fish. Rare.

Dalmatian Pelican *Pelecanus crispus* 168 cm 65 in. Same habitat and behaviour as white pelican and inhabits same areas. Rare.

Cormorant *Phalacrocorax carbo* 91 cm 36 in. Found at seashores and on inland waters. Flies low over water but settles on surface before diving for fish. Often perches with wings outspread, probably to dry them. Atlantic form is found in Britain, Norway and Iceland and breeds on rocky cliffs. Continental form is found on mainland Europe and nests in trees and bushes.

Shag *Phalacrocorax aristotelis* 76 cm 30 in. Identical to cormorant in behaviour, but smaller in size and rarely seen inland. Breeds on rocky cliffs at coast.

Pygmy Cormorant *Phalacrocorax pygmaeus* 48 cm 19 in. Usually found on inland waters. Nests in trees and bushes.

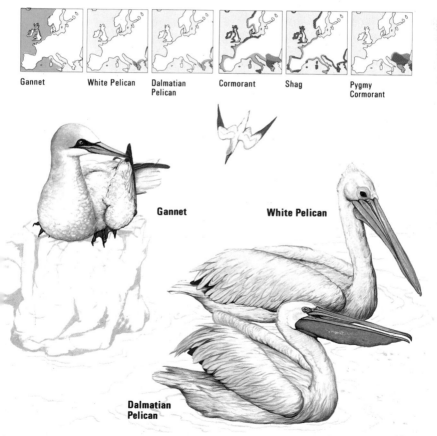

Gannet · White Pelican · Dalmatian Pelican · Cormorant · Shag · Pygmy Cormorant

Gannet

White Pelican

Dalmatian Pelican

HERON AND ALLIES

Order Ciconiiformes

These birds are elegant long-legged waders. They feed mainly in shallow water, lowering their long necks and bills to catch aquatic animals. Some herons spread their wings while fishing, perhaps to cut out the reflection of the sky. Herons and bitterns (family Ardeidae) and storks (family Ciconiidae) all have straight bills. They can easily be identified in flight because herons and bitterns draw back their heads whereas storks fly with necks outstretched. Ibises, spoonbills and flamingos have bills of unusual shapes.

Purple Heron

Grey Heron

Grey Heron *Ardea cinerea* 91 cm 36 in. The most common and largest European heron. Found on inland waters and at seashore, where it stands motionless in or near water then suddenly darts head down after prey. Also perches in trees, where it usually nests in colonies.

Purple Heron *Ardea purpurea* 79 cm 31 in. Found in swamps and marshes, where it breeds in colonies among reed-beds and bushes.

Little Egret *Egretta garzetta* 58 cm 23 in. May be found at shallow water of any kind. Usually nests near water. In summer develops hanging plumes, for which it was once hunted.

Great White Egret *Egretta alba* 89 cm 35 in. Found at shallow water; nests in reed-beds. Resembles little egret but is much larger and less common.

Squacco Heron *Ardeola ralloides* 46 cm 18 in. Found in marshes and swamps and at small stretches of water, where it nests among reeds or in bushes or trees. It is like a bittern in shape but is much less shy.

Night Heron *Nycticorax nycticorax* 61 cm 24 in. Usually seen feeding at dusk in pools and marshes, or roosting in bushes and trees during the day. Nests among reeds, bushes or trees.

Night Heron

Squacco Heron

Great White Egret

summer

winter

Little Egret

WHAT TO LOOK FOR

Grey Heron   Large size; black crest; pale grey and white; black wing edges.

Purple Heron   Long S-shaped chestnut neck with black stripe; reddish underparts.

Little Egret   Yellow feet; long white crest (summer only).

Great White Egret   Black feet; no summer crest.

Squacco Heron   Thick neck and stocky shape; buff body with white wings, but looks white in flight.

Night Heron   Stocky with rather short legs; black back, white breast; black cap.

Grey Heron

Purple Heron

Little Egret

Great White Egret

Squacco Heron

Night Heron

21

Little Bittern *Ixobrychus minutus* 36 cm 14 in. Hides away and nests among dense reeds and thickets near water. May escape detection by freezing stockstill.

Bittern *Botaurus stellaris* 76 cm 30 in. Same habitat and behaviour as little bittern, but much larger size. Freezes with bill pointing upwards. Foghorn-like booming call may be heard at a great distance.

White Stork *Ciconia ciconia* 102 cm 40 in. Found in marshes, farmland and open country. Nests on buildings, often on special platforms, or in trees near farms and villages. Walks slowly over ground.

Black Stork *Ciconia nigra* 96 cm 38 in. Frequents marshes and pools among forests, where it nests in trees. Uncommon.

Spoonbill *Platalea leucorodia* 86 cm 34 in. Found in reedy marshes, shallow lakes and estuaries. Nests in colonies

A pair of white storks. These birds often nest on buildings, and this pair have built their nest on a chimney cowling.

Little Bittern   Bittern   White Stork   Black Stork

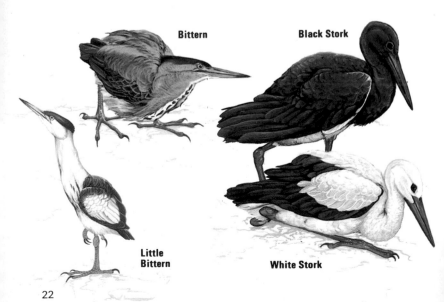

Bittern

Black Stork

Little Bittern

White Stork

among reeds or in bushes or trees. The odd spoon-shaped bill is used to sift small animals from the water. Uncommon.

Glossy Ibis *Plegadis falcinellus* 56 cm 22 in. Inhabits marshes and mudflats; nests in groups in reeds, bushes or trees, often with herons and egrets. The glossy play of colour can only be seen at close range; from a distance the plumage appears black. Uncommon.

Greater Flamingo *Phoenicopterus ruber* 125 cm 50 in. Found in flocks only in the nature reserves at the Camargue region in southern France, where it breeds, and at the Coto de Doñana in southern Spain, where breeding is rare. Single birds seen in the wild have probably escaped from collections. Wades in shallow water, dipping its bill to strain tiny creatures from the water, and nests on mudflats or on heaps of mud in water.

Spoonbill

Glossy Ibis

Greater Flamingo

Spoonbill   Glossy Ibis   Greater Flamingo

WHAT TO LOOK FOR

Little Bittern Small size; black wings with buff patch, black back (male) or brown back (female).

Bittern Large stocky shape; in freezing posture has upward-pointing bill; booming call.

White Stork White neck and upperparts; red bill and legs.

Black Stork Black neck and upperparts.

Spoonbill Long black spoon-shaped bill (pink in young bird).

Glossy Ibis Long down-curving bill.

Greater Flamingo Large bent bill; very long neck and legs; pink and black wings (in flight).

WATERFOWL OR WILDFOWL

Order Anseriformes Family Anatidae

This group of birds consists of ducks, geese and swans. They are all water birds, and use their webbed feet to swim strongly. The young are born with feathers and can walk and swim soon after hatching. Many species can be seen on lakes in parks as well as in the wild.

male

female

Mallard

DUCKS

Teal

female

male

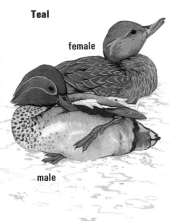

Ducks are usually smaller in size and have shorter necks than geese and swans. In addition, the two sexes have different plumage, although in late summer the drakes (males) moult and for a time resemble the ducks (females). Ducks nest on the ground or in holes. There are three main groups of ducks. *Surface-feeding* or *dabbling ducks* live in shallow water, where they feed on water plants by dabbling or up-ending. They leap into the air to get airborne, and have a brightly coloured patch of glossy wing feathers called a *speculum*. The colour of the speculum is important in identifying the drably coloured females. *Diving ducks* dive from the surface for water plants and animals, and so prefer deeper water than do dabbling ducks. Their legs are set farther back so that they can swim underwater, and they run along the surface to take wing. The third group of ducks, the *sawbills*, are also divers but have thin bills with saw-tooth edges to grip slippery fish.

Mallard *Anas platyrhynchos* 58 cm 23 in. Dabbling duck. A very common duck, found on all kinds of inland waters and at coasts and estuaries. Often seen in flocks. Most domestic ducks, though different in colour, are descended from wild mallards.

Teal *Anas crecca* 36 cm 14 in. Dabbling duck. Smallest European duck. Prefers secluded inland waters in summer; spreads to open waters and coast in winter.

Garganey *Anas querquedula* 38 cm 15 in. Dabbling duck. Prefers inland waters.

Gadwall *Anas strepera* 51 cm 20 in. Dabbling duck. Prefers inland waters.

Wigeon *Anas penelope* 46 cm 18 in. Dabbling duck. Prefers inland waters in summer; spreads to coast in winter, when it may be seen in flocks. May graze on land.

WHAT TO LOOK FOR

Mallard   Male: dark green head; chestnut breast. Female: blue-purple speculum.

Teal   Male: brown and green head. Female: small size; green speculum.

Garganey   Male: white stripe on head. Female: blue-grey forewing; indistinct speculum.

Gadwall   Male: grey body with black rear; brown wing panel; black and white speculum. Female: white belly; black and white speculum.

Wigeon   Male: chestnut head with light crown; white forewing. Female: black and green speculum; white belly.

Garganey — female, male

Wigeon — female, male

Gadwall — female, male

Mallard   Teal   Garganey

Gadwall   Wigeon

A male mandarin duck. This species is usually seen in parks.

Pintail *Anas acuta* 63 cm 25 in. Dabbling duck. Prefers inland waters in summer, but coasts in winter.

Shoveler *Anas clypeata* 51 cm 20 in. Dabbling duck. Usually found on ponds and in marshes. The odd-shaped bill, unlike that of all other ducks, is used to strain tiny plants and animals from the water.

Mandarin Duck *Aix galericulata* 46 cm 18 in. Dabbling duck. Introduced from China and seen mainly on park lakes. Nests in tree holes. Escaped birds live in the wild, preferring ponds surrounded by trees.

Red–crested Pochard *Netta rufina* 56 cm 22 in. Diving duck. Prefers inland waters. Uncommon.

Scaup *Aythya marila* 46 cm 18 in. Diving duck. Breeds inland, but otherwise seen at coast and estuaries.

Tufted Duck *Aythya fuligula* 43 cm 17 in. Diving duck. Often seen on lakes and ponds; also at seashore and estuaries in winter.

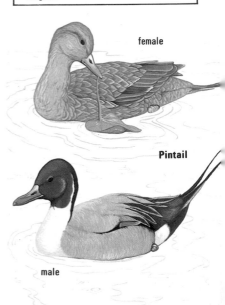

female

Pintail

male

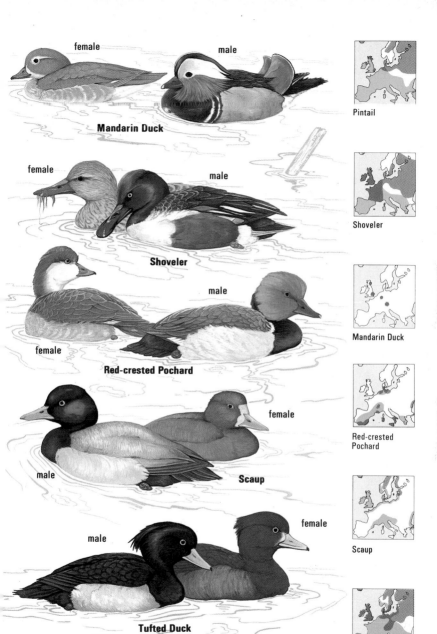

female male
Mandarin Duck

Pintail

female male
Shoveler

Shoveler

male
female
Red-crested Pochard

Mandarin Duck

female
male
Scaup

Red-crested
Pochard

female
male
Tufted Duck

Scaup

Tufted Duck

female   male

Pochard

female

male   **Goldeneye**

female

male

Ferruginous Duck

Pochard   Ferruginous   Goldeneye
           Duck

Pochard *Aythya ferina* 46 cm 18 in.
Diving duck. Breeds among reeds,
otherwise seen mainly on lakes and at
estuaries.
Ferruginous Duck *Aythya nyroca*
41 cm 16 in. Diving duck. Breeds
among reeds on inland waters; winters
at open inland waters, rarely at coast.
Goldeneye *Bucephala clangula* 46 cm
18 in. Diving duck. Nests in tree
holes and burrows near fresh water;
winters on lakes, rivers and coastal
waters. Drakes raise bill in courting
display in early spring. Wings whistle
in flight.
Long–tailed Duck *Clangula hyemalis*
51 cm 20 in (female 41 cm 16 in).
Diving duck. Breeds in the Arctic;
winters on coastal waters.
Velvet Scoter *Melanitta fusca* 56 cm
22 in. Diving duck. Usually breeds
on inland waters; winters at coast and
on large lakes.
Common Scoter *Melanitta nigra*
51 cm 20 in. Breeds on islands as well
as inland; winters mainly at coast.

female (summer)

male (summer)

Velvet Scoter

Common Scoter

Long-tailed
Duck

Velvet Scoter

Common Scoter

Pochard Male: dark chestnut head and neck with pale grey back; black breast. Female: brown head with light stripe through eye; blue band on bill; grey wing band.

Ferruginous Duck Male: rich brown head, neck and breast; white eye; white patch under tail; bold white wingbar. Female: as male, but dull brown and brown eye; white patch under tail and white wingbar.

Goldeneye Male: round white patch before eye. Female: brown head with white collar.

Long-tailed Duck Male: long pointed tail; dark head and neck with white face patch (summer) or white head and neck with dark neck patch (winter). Female: white face and belly with dark back, shoulders and wings.

Velvet Scoter Male: all black except for white patch below eye and white wingbar. Female: two light patches on each side of head; white wingbar.

Common Scoter Male: all black except for orange patch on bill; black knob above bill. Female: dark cap; light cheek.

Long-tailed Duck

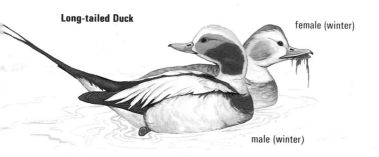

female (winter)

male (winter)

Eider *Somateria mollissima* 61 cm 24 in. Diving duck. Most marine of all ducks, seldom found inland. Breeds at seashore, lining nest with soft breast feathers known as eider down.

White–headed Duck *Oxyura leucocephala* 46 cm 18 in. Diving duck. Confined to inland waters. Often points tail upwards when swimming. Uncommon.

Red–breasted Merganser *Mergus serrator* 56 cm 22 in. Sawbill (see page 24). Breeds near fresh or salt water, hiding nest among rocks or vegetation. Mainly found at coasts in winter.

Goosander *Mergus merganser* 66 cm 26 in. Sawbill. Nests in tree cavities and burrows near fresh water. Usually remains inland in winter.

Smew *Mergus albellus* 41 cm 16 in. Sawbill (but duck-like appearance). Nests in holes in trees near inland waters. Also found at coast in winter.

Shelduck *Tadorna tadorna* 61 cm 24 in. Large goose-like duck. Nests in hollow trees and burrows or among bushes. Winters mainly at coasts, often on mudflats. Sexes almost identical.

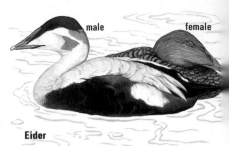

male female

Eider

Eider   White-headed Duck   Red-breasted Merganser

Goosander   Smew   Shelduck

Goosander nesting in tree cavity

Goosander

female male

female

male

White-headed Duck

Smew

female

male

male

female

Shelduck

Red-breasted Merganser

female

male

31

GEESE

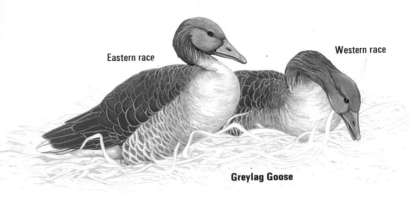

Eastern race

Western race

Greylag Goose

Geese are between ducks and swans in size. They graze mainly on land, and the legs are set forward so that they can walk easily. The sexes are alike. There are two groups of geese. Geese of the genus *Anser* are grey-brown and those of the genus *Branta* are black and white.

Greenland race

Main race

White-fronted Goose

Greylag Goose *Anser anser* 84 cm 33 in. Very common goose. Breeds on moors, marshes, reedy lakes, and offshore islands. Winters in fields, inland and coastal marshes and at estuaries. There are two subspecies, or races. The western race (*A.a. anser*) is found in Iceland, Britain and western Europe; the eastern race (*A.a. rubrirostris*) inhabits eastern Europe. All domestic geese are descended from the greylag goose.

White-fronted Goose *Anser albifrons* 71 cm 28 in. Found in same habitat as greylag goose in winter, but breeds in far north. There are two subspecies. The Greenland race (*A.a. flavirostris*) migrates from Greenland to winter in Ireland and western Scotland. The main, or typical, race (*A.a. albifrons*) breeds in northern Russia and winters in the rest of Britain and mainland Europe.

Lesser White-fronted Goose *Anser erythropus* 61 cm 24 in. Similar habitat and appearance to white-fronted goose, but smaller size.

Bean Goose *Anser fabalis* 76 cm 30 in. Breeds in northern woods and tundra; winters inland in fields near water.

Pink-footed Goose *Anser brachyrhynchus* 68 cm 27 in. Breeds in Arctic; similar winter habitat to bean goose.

Domestic greylag geese.

Bean Goose

Lesser White-fronted Goose

Pink-footed Goose

Greylag Goose

White-fronted Goose

Lesser White-fronted Goose

Bean Goose

Pink-footed Goose

33

Brent Goose *Branta bernicla* 58 cm 23 in. Winter visitor to coasts and estuaries. Feeds mainly on eel grasses in water, and feeding times depend on tides. There are two subspecies. The light-bellied form (*B.b. hrota*) breeds in Greenland and Spitsbergen, and the dark-bellied form (*B.b. bernicla*) in northern Russia.

Barnacle Goose *Branta leucopsis* 63 cm 25 in. Winter visitor from Arctic to salt marshes and estuaries and surrounding fields. The odd name comes from a medieval belief that the birds hatch from goose barnacles instead of eggs.

Canada Goose *Branta canadensis* 97 cm 38 in. Largest European goose. Introduced from North America to parks. Escaped birds now breed in Britain and Sweden, and may migrate to western Europe for the winter. Wild birds nest on islands in lakes and graze in marshes and fields by lakes and rivers.

WHAT TO LOOK FOR

Brent Goose   Black head and neck with small white neck mark.

Barnacle Goose   White face, black neck and breast.

Canada Goose   Long black neck, black head with white throat, light breast.

Barnacle Goose   Brent Goose

Canada Goose

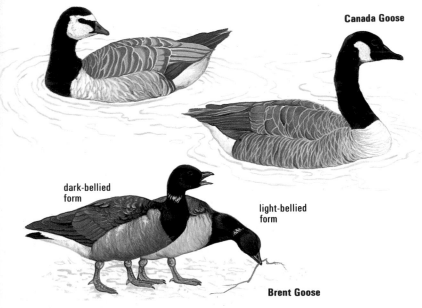

Barnacle Goose

Canada Goose

dark-bellied form

light-bellied form

Brent Goose

SWANS

Mute Swan

Bewjck's Swan

Whooper Swan

Whooper Swan

Mute Swan

Bewick's Swan

WHAT TO LOOK FOR

Mute Swan Orange bill with black knob; neck usually curved.

Whooper Swan Large size; yellow bill with black tip; neck usually straight.

Bewick's Swan Small size; black bill with yellow base; neck usually straight.

Swans are the largest waterfowl and immediately recognised by their long elegant necks, which they lower into the water or to the ground to pull up plants. The sexes are alike. The black swan seen in parks has been introduced from Australia. The birds should be approached with caution, especially when breeding.

Mute Swan *Cygnus olor* 152 cm 60 in. Very common. Often found in tame state on park lakes and village ponds and along rivers. Usually nests at banks of rivers and lakes; winters on open waters and at coast.

Whooper Swan *Cygnus cygnus* 152 cm 60 in. Nests in swamps and by lakes in far north; winters along coasts and on lakes and rivers. Its name refers to whooping sound of call.

Bewick's Swan *Cygnus bewickii* 122 cm 48 in. Winter visitors from Arctic. Similar habitat to whooper swan, though prefers larger areas of water in more open country.

BIRDS OF PREY

Order Falconiformes

The birds of prey hunt other animals. Usually they catch live prey on the ground, in the air or in water, but sometimes they eat dead animals. Other birds, such as owls and crows, also feed in these ways, but the birds of prey are different in that they all have sharp claws to grip their victims and hooked beaks to tear them to pieces. Also, unlike most owls, birds of prey hunt by day and not by night.

Golden Eagle

Griffon Vulture

Lammergeyer

Black Vulture

Griffon Vulture

Egyptian Vulture

Black Vulture

Egyptian Vulture

Spanish form

Imperial Eagle

VULTURES, EAGLES, BUZZARDS, HAWKS, KITES AND HARRIERS

Family Accipitridae

Most of these birds of prey soar through the air, keeping a sharp lookout for prey below and then dropping on an unsuspecting victim. However, vultures land on the ground to feed on carrion (dead animals) and on refuse. Eagles mainly seek live prey as they soar. Buzzards and kites also soar and look rather like small eagles, though buzzards may also be seen perching and kites can be told by their long forked tails. Hawks and harriers fly near the ground, hawks dashing rapidly through the air and harriers gliding gently.

WHAT TO LOOK FOR

Egyptian Vulture Long thin bill with bare yellow skin on face; white plumage with black wingtips.

Griffon Vulture White neck and head with white ruff.

Black Vulture Dark patches on head and long bare neck with dark ruff.

Lammergeyer Long narrow wings and long diamond-shaped tail; orange breast.

Golden Eagle Dark brown all over with golden feathers on head.

Imperial Eagle White shoulders; white wing patches (Spanish form only).

Lammergeyer   Golden Eagle   Imperial Eagle

Egyptian Vulture *Neophron percnopterus* 63 cm 25 in. Usually seen in mountains, but comes to rubbish dumps in villages. In Africa, it is well known for its habit of dropping stones on ostrich eggs to break them open.

Griffon Vulture *Gyps fulvus* 100 cm 39 in. Usually found in mountains. Unlike eagles, has head and tail that appear very small in flight.

Black Vulture *Aegypius monachus* 102 cm 40 in. Usually found in mountains and plains, but rare. If all three vultures arrive at a carcass together, the black vulture feeds first, then the griffon vulture and finally the Egyptian vulture.

Lammergeyer or **Bearded Vulture** *Gypaetus barbatus* 110 cm 43 in. Found in mountains; does not join other vultures to feed. Known for unusual habit of dropping bones from the air to rocks to break them open.

Golden Eagle *Aquila chrysaetos* 84 cm 33 in. Usually seen soaring above mountain slopes, though may hunt near the ground. May also be found at coasts and in woods and fields. Nests in trees or on rock ledges.

Imperial Eagle *Aquila heliaca* 81 cm 32 in. Found in low-lying forests, woods, plains and marshes. Nests in tall trees.

Bonelli's Eagle

light form

Short-toed Eagle

dark form

Booted Eagle

dark form

light form

Bonelli's Eagle *Hieraaetus fasciatus* 71 cm 28 in. Usually found in mountains, but may also be seen in more open country in winter. Dashes rapidly through the air, hunting for small mammals and birds. Nests in trees and on rock ledges.

Booted Eagle *Hieraaetus pennatus* 51 cm 20 in. Usually found in forests or woods, hunting in clearings. Nests in trees. Plumage varies from light to dark, but light birds are more common than dark birds.

Short–toed Eagle *Circaetus gallicus* 66 cm 26 in. Found in mountains and gorges, plains and woods and at coasts. Often hovers, seeking snakes, lizards and frogs. Nests in trees. Head plumage may be light or dark, dark being more common.

Buzzard *Buteo buteo* 53 cm 21 in. Found in woods, fields and plains, at coasts and on mountain slopes and hillsides. Often soars, but hunts near the ground. Nests in trees and on rock ledges. Plumage varies from cream to dark brown.

Rough–legged Buzzard *Buteo lagopus* 56 cm 22 in. Found in winter on moors and in marshes and fields, in summer among mountains. Nests on cliff ledges or on ground in Arctic. Often hovers before swooping on small mammals; also hunts birds.

Sparrowhawk *Accipiter nisus* 33 cm 13 in. Usually seen in forests and woods, but also among scattered trees and bushes. Dashes through trees and hops over hedges, hunting small birds. Female is much larger than male. Nests in trees and bushes.

Goshawk *Accipiter gentilis* 53 cm 21 in. Usually seen in woods and forests, dashing through trees in pursuit of birds. Nests mainly in fir trees. Resembles female sparrowhawk, but much bigger. Female is larger than male.

Buzzard

light form

dark form

Rough-legged Buzzard

Goshawk

female

male

Sparrowhawk

Bonelli's Eagle

Booted Eagle

Short-toed Eagle

Buzzard

Rough-legged Buzzard

Sparrowhawk

Goshawk

WHAT TO LOOK FOR

Bonelli's Eagle White underparts; wings dark above or white with dark band beneath.

Booted Eagle Small size like buzzard but long narrow tail.

Short-toed Eagle White underparts with white underwings and often dark breast and head.

Buzzard Like small golden eagle but broad rounded tail.

Rough-legged Buzzard Dark belly; white tail with black band at tip.

Sparrowhawk Broad rounded wings with long tail; closely barred underparts.

Goshawk Both sexes similar to sparrowhawk but larger size.

Red Kite *Milvus milvus* 63 cm 25 in. Usually found in woods, but also among scattered trees. Nests in trees.

Black Kite *Milvus migrans* 53 cm 21 in. Usually seen near lakes and rivers surrounded by trees. In southern Europe, also found in more open country and seeking refuse in towns and villages. Nests in trees.

White–tailed Eagle or **Sea Eagle** *Haliaeetus albicilla* 81 cm 32 in. Found at coasts and remote lakes. Takes fish from surface of water or plunges; also hunts mammals and birds. Nests in trees and on rock ledges.

Honey Buzzard *Pernis apivorus* 53 cm 21 in. Usually found in clearings and at edges of forests and woods. Gets its name from its habit of feeding at the nests of bees and wasps, though for grubs and not for honey. Nests in trees. Colour varies from cream to dark brown.

Marsh Harrier *Circus aeruginosus* 51 cm 20 in. Usually seen flying low over swamps and marshes and nearby fields. Nests in reed-beds.

Hen Harrier *Circus cyaneus* 46 cm 18 in. Hunts while flying low over moors, heaths, fields, pasture, marshes and swamps. Makes its nest on the ground.

Montagu's Harrier *Circus pygargus* 43 cm 17 in. Found in same places and has similar flight and nesting habits to hen harrier.

Red Kite   Black Kite   White-tailed Eagle   Honey Buzzard   Marsh Harrier   Hen Harrier

Red Kite

White-tailed Eagle

Black Kite

Honey Buzzard

female

male

Marsh Harrier

OSPREYS

Family Pandionidae

The osprey differs slightly from all other birds of prey and is in a family by itself.

Osprey *Pandion haliaetus* 56 cm 22 in. Found on lakes and rivers and at coast, where it hunts fish by soaring or hovering high over the water and then plunging in feet-first. Carries fish back to perch near water.

Osprey

female

Hen Harrier

male

A female Montagu's harrier arriving at her nest.

Montagu's Harrier   Osprey

Montagu's Harrier

male

female

WHAT TO LOOK FOR

Red Kite Like buzzard, but reddish colour and deeply forked tail.

Black Kite As red kite, but dark plumage and shallow forked tail.

White-tailed Eagle White tail with brown body.

Honey Buzzard Like buzzard, but longer tail with black bands.

Marsh Harrier Male: grey wing patch and tail. Female: pale crown and throat.

Hen Harrier Male: grey with white rump and underside. Female: streaky brown with white rump (very like Montagu's harrier).

Montagu's Harrier Male: as male hen harrier but black wingbar, grey rump and streaky underside. Female: very similar to female hen harrier.

Osprey Dark above and white below, with white head crossed by dark line.

Peregrine Falcon

Hobby

Lanner Falcon

Gyrfalcon

FALCONS

Family Falconidae

Falcons are generally smaller than other birds of prey, and have long, pointed wings and long tails. They are ferocious hunters, diving on or chasing their prey at great speed. Falconers train falcons to hunt and bring their prey back to them. Female falcons are usually larger than male falcons.

Hobby

Peregrine Falcon | Gyrfalcon | Lanner Falcon | Merlin | Lesser Kestrel | Kestrel

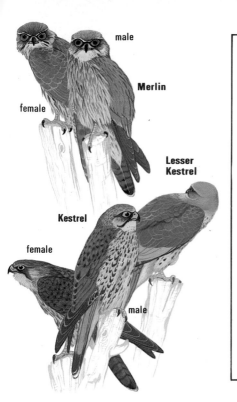

male

Merlin

female

Lesser
Kestrel

Kestrel

female

male

Hobby *Falco subbuteo* 33 cm 13 in. Lives in light woodland and among scattered trees, streaking through the air in pursuit of small birds such as larks, swallows and swifts, as well as flying insects. Nests in trees.

Peregrine Falcon *Falco peregrinus* 43 cm 17 in. Found among cliffs and crags, on which it nests, and also at flat coasts and marshes in winter; sometimes seen in forests and towns. Hunts by diving steeply at great speed, wings drawn back, mainly after birds, especially pigeons. Has become rare, suffering badly from effects of pesticides and raids by egg collectors.

Gyrfalcon *Falco rusticolus* 53 cm 21 in. Found in mountains and at coasts and forest edges. Nests on cliff ledges. Hunts like peregrine falcon but is not so fast in flight.

Lanner Falcon *Falco biarmicus* 43 cm 17 in. Found in mountains and rocky open country and at shores. Nests in rocks and trees. Flight similar to peregrine falcon, but preys on smaller birds.

Merlin *Falco columbarius* 30 cm 12 in. Found in open country, on hills and moors in summer and also at coast in winter. Nests on ground or in trees. Darts through the air close to the ground, chasing small birds. May be seen hovering and perching.

Lesser Kestrel *Falco naumanni* 30 cm 12 in. Found in open and rocky country and marshes, and often in fields around towns and villages. Nests on cliffs and buildings. Resembles kestrel, but does not hover so often.

Kestrel *Falco tinnunculus* 33 cm 13 in. Very common bird of prey. Found in all kinds of places, including cities and towns; often spotted alongside motorways. Usually seen hovering near ground, flapping wings quickly, and then diving down in pursuit of rodents and insects.

GAME BIRDS OR FOWLS
Order Galliformes

These birds are plump in shape, rather like chickens. They rarely fly very far or high and prefer to run or hide from danger, only taking to the air at the last moment. They spend most of their time on the ground rooting for seeds and insects, and they also nest on the ground. They are called game birds because most of them are hunted for sport, although hunting is forbidden when the birds are nesting and raising their young.

female

male

Hazelhen

GROUSE
Family Tetraonidae

These birds live in cold places, and their legs and sometimes their feet are covered with feathers for warmth.

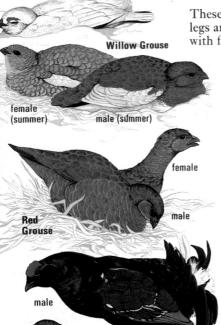

male
(winter)

female
(winter)

Willow Grouse

female
(summer)

male (summer)

female

male

**Red
Grouse**

male

female   **Black Grouse**

Willow Grouse *Lagopus lagopus* 38 cm 15 in. Found on moors, often living among heather and scattered bushes. Plumage changes from white in winter to brown and white in summer, helping to hide bird among winter snow and summer plants.
Red Grouse *Lagopus lagopus scoticus* 38 cm 15 in. A variety of willow grouse found only in the British Isles. No colour change takes place because snow does not always fall in winter. Lives among heather on moors, but also found in fields in winter.
Ptarmigan *Lagopus mutus* 36 cm 14 in. Found on high mountain slopes, usually above tree level. Plumage changes from brown and white in summer to grey and white in autumn

Willow Grouse   Red Grouse   Ptarmigan

44

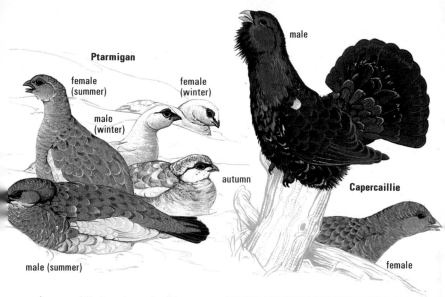

Ptarmigan

female (summer)

female (winter)

male (winter)

male (winter)

autumn

male (summer)

male

Capercaillie

female

and pure white in winter. In this way, it always matches its surroundings and cannot easily be spotted by an eagle or a fox.

Black Grouse *Lyrurus tetrix* Male 53 cm 21 in; female 41 cm 16 in. Found on moors, in woods, among scattered trees and in fields. In spring, groups gather at courting grounds and the males display themselves before the females, spreading their wings and raising their white tail feathers in a fan.

Capercaillie *Tetrao urogallus* Male 86 cm 34 in; female 61 cm 24 in. Lives among fir trees on hills and mountains. Male raises tail in a fan when courting female.

Hazelhen or **Hazel Grouse** *Tetrastes bonasia* 36 cm 14 in. Lives in woods, usually hiding among bushes and thickets, but takes to the air when disturbed.

WHAT TO LOOK FOR

Willow Grouse Male: in summer, red-brown body with white wings and belly; in winter, pure white with black tail (but exactly like female ptarmigan). Female: in summer, as male, but body less red and more barred; in winter, as male.

Red Grouse Male: red-brown body with dark wings and tail edges. Female: as male, but body less red and more barred.

Ptarmigan Male: as willow grouse, but greyer body in summer and autumn, and black face patch in winter. Female: very like female willow grouse, but usually found at higher altitudes.

Black Grouse Male: glossy black with lyre-shaped tail. Female: grey-brown with slightly forked tail.

Capercaillie Male: grey with broad fan-shaped tail; brownish wings. Female: as female black grouse, but with fan-shaped tail and reddish breast patch.

Hazelhen Male: black throat and grey tail with black band. Female: as male but whitish throat.

Black Grouse

Capercaillie

Hazelhen

45

PARTRIDGES AND PHEASANTS

Family Phasianidae

Unlike grouse, these birds have bare legs and feet and are not found in cold places. Brightly coloured pheasants from other parts of the world are seen in parks. Some now live in the wild. Pheasants make their nests on the ground and produce large numbers of young birds. Partridges too nest on the ground and are difficult to see. They are not good fliers and do not migrate. Quails are small shy birds prized as a delicacy.

Rock Partridge *Alectoris graeca* 33 cm 13 in. Found on rocky ground and among trees, usually high up. Looks very like red-legged partridge, but lives in different countries.

Red–legged Partridge *Alectoris rufa* 34 cm 13½ in. Found on moors, and in fields and low treeless hills, often in dry and stony places. Looks like rock partridge, but lives in different countries.

Partridge *Perdix perdix* 30 cm 12 in. Seen mainly in fields, but also on

female
male
Quail

Rock Partridge

Red-legged Partridge

male
female

Partridge

WHAT TO LOOK FOR

Rock Partridge   Red legs; white throat patch surrounded by solid black band.

Red-legged Partridge   Like rock partridge, but with black streaks below breast band.

Partridge   Grey legs; orange-brown face and throat; dark belly patch (male only).

Quail   Small size; striped head; dark throat patch (male only).

Pheasant   Male: very long tail with green head and red eye patch. Female: mottled brown body with long pointed tail.

46

The spectacular colouring of its crest gives the golden pheasant its name. It is a native of central Asia and China, like the ring-necked pheasant, which has a characteristic white ring around its throat, and the beautiful Chinese silver pheasant, with its delicate black markings on its back. These exotic relatives of the European pheasants are found only in parks.

male

female

Pheasant

moors and heaths and in marshes, sand dunes and low treeless hills.

Quail *Coturnix coturnix* 18 cm 7 in. The smallest European game bird, and the only one that migrates. Hides among grass and crops.

Pheasant *Phasianus colchicus* Male 84 cm 33 in; female 58 cm 23 in. Often seen in fields, especially in winter; also in woods and marshes. Pattern of male varies; for example some have white neck-ring while others do not.

Rock
Partridge

Red-legged
Partridge

Partridge

Quail

Pheasant

47

Water Rail

Crane

A male little crake at the nest.

CRANES, RAILS AND BUSTARDS
Order Gruiformes

All these birds have long legs and many of them wade in shallow water. Cranes (family Gruidae) are tall, elegant birds living on dry land and in marshes, whereas rails, crakes, gallinules, moorhens and coots (family Rallidae) are mainly water birds, small to medium in size and chunky in shape. Bustards (family Otididae) are land birds, medium to large in size with long thick necks.

Spotted Crake

Baillon's Crake

female

male

Little Crake

Corncrake

Crane *Grus grus* 114 cm 45 in. Nests on the ground in swamps and among reeds; in winter moves to rivers, fields and plains. Told from storks and herons by bushy tail. Flies with neck outstretched, migrating in long lines or V-formations. In spring, cranes perform crazy leaping dances before nesting.

Water Rail *Rallus aquaticus* 28 cm 11 in. Usually hides among reeds in marshes and ponds, and nests on concealed platform of reeds built above water. Likely to come into the open during cold weather.

Spotted Crake *Porzana porzana* 23 cm 9 in. Location and behaviour similar to water rail, but even more shy.

Baillon's Crake *Porzana pusilla* 18 cm 7 in. Same location and behaviour as water rail, and similar appearance but much smaller. Very shy.

Little Crake *Porzana parva* 19 cm 7½ in. Same location and behaviour as water rail but much smaller; male is very like Baillon's crake in appearance. Very shy.

Corncrake or **Land Rail** *Crex crex* 25 cm 10 in. Hides away and nests among long grass and crops in meadows and fields. Mowing machines and other changes in agriculture have caused a drop in numbers.

WHAT TO LOOK FOR

Crane Red crown and white cheek stripe; bushy drooping tail.

Water Rail Long red beak.

Spotted Crake Dark brown spotted and streaky plumage.

Baillon's Crake Grey underside with bars on flanks; flesh-coloured legs.

Little Crake Male: as Baillon's crake, but no bars on flanks and green legs. Female: as male, but buff underside.

Corncrake Buff plumage with reddish wing patches.

Crane

Water Rail

Spotted Crake

Baillon's Crake

Little Crake

Corncrake

Purple Gallinule *Porphyrio porphyrio* 48 cm 19 in. Lives and nests among reed-beds in swamps and lakes.

Moorhen *Gallinula chloropus* 33 cm 13 in. Lives on ponds, lakes and streams, bobbing its head up and down as it swims to and fro and sometimes diving for food. Often seen in parks. Nests in reeds, bushes and trees, usually near the water. Often feeds on grassy banks and in nearby fields.

Coot *Fulica atra* 38 cm 15 in. Found on lakes, reservoirs and rivers, and in parks. Also at coast in winter. Prefers larger stretches of water than does moorhen, and dives more often. Usually seen in groups, with the birds always quarrelling. Nests in reeds and plants at water's edge.

Great Bustard *Otis tarda* Male 102 cm 40 in; female 76 cm 30 in. Lives on plains and in fields, where it also nests. May be seen walking through grass with head upright, but is very shy. Males court females by bending themselves into contortions to display fans of white feathers. Hunting in past reduced numbers and is now rare.

Little Bustard *Otis tetrax* 43 cm 17 in. Same location and behaviour as great bustard. Hides by crouching flat when danger approaches. In winter, male looks like female.

WHAT TO LOOK FOR

Purple Gallinule Large red beak and long red legs and toes; purple-blue plumage.

Moorhen Black body with red bill and shield above bill.

Coot Black body with white bill and shield.

Great Bustard Large size; grey head and neck; moustache of long white bristles (male only).

Little Bustard Male: black and white pattern on neck (summer only). Female and male in winter: streaky brown head and neck.

Purple
Gallinule   Moorhen   Coot

Great
Bustard

Little
Bustard

Purple Gallinule

Moorhen

Coot

A coot shows its lobed toes.

Little Bustard

female   male

Courtship display of
male Great Bustard

Great Bustard   male

female

51

WADERS, GULLS AND AUKS

Order Charadriiformes

This is a huge group of many different kinds of birds, but they all spend at least part of their lives in or near water. Waders (mainly plovers and sandpipers) live at the seashore and in marshes. They have long legs so that they can walk in shallow water. Skuas, gulls, terns and auks are sea birds and have webbed feet.

OYSTERCATCHERS

Family Haematopodidae

Oystercatcher *Haematopus ostralegus* 43 cm 17 in. The only European member of its family. Seen at seashore, prising shellfish open with its chisel-like beak. Also probes for food in mud. May also be found inland on moors and by lakes and rivers.

Oystercatcher

Grey Plover

winter   summer

Golden Plover

southern form (summer)

winter

northern form (summer)

WHAT TO LOOK FOR

Oystercatcher   Black and white plumage with long red beak.

Lapwing   Black and white plumage with crest; glossy dark-green back.

Ringed Plover   Black breast band and yellow legs; white wingbar in flight.

Little Ringed Plover   As ringed plover but no wingbar and legs often pink.

Kentish Plover   As ringed plover, but breast band incomplete and black legs.

Grey Plover   Summer: black below and silver-grey above. Winter: white below and grey above.

Golden Plover   Summer: black below and golden-brown above. Winter: white below and golden-brown above.

Dotterel   White eye-stripe and breast band (pale in winter); dark underparts.

Turnstone   Summer: brown and black patterned wings. Winter: dark breast band and orange legs.

Oystercatcher   Lapwing   Ringed Plover

Lapwing

Kentish Plover

Little Ringed Plover

Ringed Plover

winter

Dotterel

summer

winter

Turnstone

summer

PLOVERS

Family Charadriidae

Plovers can be told from almost all other waders by their short beaks. They probe in soil, mud and sand, both at the seashore and inland, for worms, grubs and shell-fish. They often run about, stopping to bob their heads or tilt them at an angle, as if listening for something. All plovers nest on the ground. Many protect their young from enemies by pretending to have a broken wing and luring them away from the nest.

Lapwing, Peewit or **Green Plover** *Vanellus vanellus* 30 cm 12 in. Very common plover. Found in fields and marshes and on moors; also at coast in winter. Usually in large flocks.
Ringed Plover *Charadrius hiaticula* 19 cm 7½ in. Usually found on sandy and stony beaches, sometimes inland.
Little Ringed Plover *Charadrius dubius* 15 cm 6 in. Lives on sandy or stony shores of lakes and rivers, and in old gravel pits.
Kentish Plover *Charadrius alexandrinus* 15 cm 6 in. Found at seashore, on sandy or stony beaches.
Grey Plover *Pluvialis squatarola* 28 cm 11 in. Found on mudflats and sandy beaches.
Golden Plover *Pluvialis apricaria* 28 cm 11 in. Nests on moors in summer. In winter, also found in fields and at seashore, usually with lapwings.
Dotterel *Eudromias morinellus* 23 cm 9 in. Nests on barren high ground. In winter, found in fields and at seashores.
Turnstone *Arenaria interpres* 23 cm 9 in. Found at coast, usually on rocky and stony shores. Gets name from its habit of turning over stones, shells and seaweed when looking for food.

Little Ringed Plover

Kentish Plover

Grey Plover

Golden Plover

Dotterel

Turnstone

SANDPIPERS
Family Scolopacidae

Woodcock

Curlew

Whimbrel

Snipe

These are wading birds with long bills. Most also have long legs. They may be found inland at damp places as well as at the seashore, and they usually nest on the ground. Flocks of several different kinds of sandpipers can often be seen feeding together at the shore, poking their bills into the water, mud or sand to find shellfish and worms. The different kinds of birds have bills of various lengths, so that they probe at different depths and live on different kinds of food.

Snipe

Great Snipe

Jack Snipe

Woodcock

Curlew

Whimbrel

Black-tailed Godwit

Bar-tailed Godwit

Great Snipe

Jack Snipe

Snipe *Gallinago gallinago* 27 cm 10½ in. Hides away in marshes, bogs and damp meadows. Flies away with zigzag flight when disturbed. Often dives from sky, making a drumming noise with its tail.

Great Snipe *Gallinago media* 28 cm 11 in. Hides away in marshes or reedy river banks, especially when nesting. At other times, may also be found in fields and on heaths. Usually flies off in straight line when disturbed.

Jack Snipe *Lymnocryptes minimus* 19 cm 7½ in. Found in same places as snipe and behaves in same way, except that when disturbed it flies off with a more direct flight. Its call sounds rather like a distant galloping horse.

Woodcock *Scolopax rusticola* 36 cm 14 in. Hides away among damp woodland. Most likely to be seen at dawn or dusk flying through the trees or in circles above the trees.

Curlew *Numenius arquata* 56 cm 22 in. Nests on moors and in marshes, damp meadows and sand dunes. In winter, also seen on mudflats at seashore.

Whimbrel *Numenius phaeopus* 41 cm 16 in. Found in same places as curlew, and looks like a small curlew, but told apart by its head pattern.

Black–tailed Godwit *Limosa limosa* 41 cm 16 in. Nests in damp meadows

WHAT TO LOOK FOR

Snipe Long straight beak with dark stripes along head. Also zigzag flight.

Great Snipe As snipe, but white sides to tail and straight flight pattern.

Jack Snipe As snipe but shorter bill and pointed tail.

Woodcock Long beak with dark stripes across head. Stout shape.

Curlew Very long down-curving bill and plain head.

Whimbrel As curlew, but shorter bill and striped head.

Black-tailed Godwit Summer: long bill (very slightly upturned) with chestnut breast and white tail with black band at end. Winter: as summer but grey breast.

Bar-tailed Godwit As black-tailed godwit, but upturned bill and barred tail.

and on boggy land. In winter, also seen on mudflats and in marshes.

Bar–tailed Godwit *Limosa lapponica* 38 cm 15 in. Nests in marshes in Arctic and migrates to spend winter at seashore.

summer   Bar-tailed Godwit

winter

winter

Black-tailed Godwit   summer

Green Sandpiper

Green Sandpiper *Tringa ochropus* 23 cm 9 in. Nests in swamps in woodland. Winters in marshes and on lakes and rivers, seldom at coast.

Wood Sandpiper *Tringa glareola* 20 cm 8 in. Found in northern forests and in Arctic, where it nests on ground near water and in old nests in trees.

Common Sandpiper *Tringa hypoleucos* 20 cm 8 in. Nests beside streams, rivers and lakes, usually in hills. In winter, also seen at seashore. Bobs its tail and nods its head as it wades.

Redshank *Tringa totanus* 28 cm 11 in. Nests among grass in meadows and inland and coastal marshes and on moors and heaths. In winter, usually found at seashore.

Spotted Redshank *Tringa erythropus* 30 cm 12 in. Nests in far north and migrates to spend winter at seashore and in marshes.

Greenshank *Tringa nebularia* 30 cm 12 in. Nests on ground on moors or in forests, usually near water. In winter, seen at seashore and on inland waters.

Wood Sandpiper

Common Sandpiper

WHAT TO LOOK FOR

Green Sandpiper White rump with dark legs, no wingbar. Not green.

Wood Sandpiper White rump with pale legs, no wingbar.

Common Sandpiper Dark rump, white wingbar seen in flight; bobs tail.

Redshank White rump with long red legs; white band at back of wing in flight.

Spotted Redshank Summer: black with red legs, no wingband. Winter: pale grey with red legs, no wingband.

Greenshank White rump with greenish legs; no wingband.

Green Sandpiper

Wood Sandpiper

Common Sandpiper

Redshank

Spotted Redshank

Greenshank

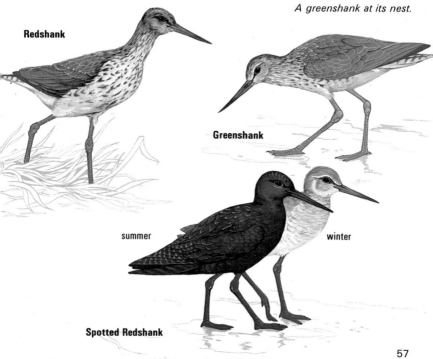

A greenshank at its nest.

Redshank

Greenshank

summer

winter

Spotted Redshank

summer
Knot

winter

Curlew
Sandpiper

winter

summer

summer

winter

Purple
Sandpiper

winter

summer

winter

Little
Stint

summer

winter

Sanderling

summer

winter

Temminck's
Stint

summer

winter

summer

Dunlin

Knot *Calidris canutus* 25 cm 10 in. A winter visitor from the Arctic. Seen at mudflats along seashores, often in flocks. Birds in summer plumage may be seen in spring and autumn.

Purple Sandpiper *Calidris maritima* 20 cm 8 in. Found at rocky shores and harbours in winter. Nests among low plants in far north. Back has purple gloss, but this can be seen only in bright light.

Little Stint *Calidris minuta* 13 cm 5 in. Nests in Arctic and winters in Africa. During migration in spring and autumn may be seen throughout Europe on mudflats at coasts and inland on reservoirs, lakes and sewage farms.

Temminck's Stint *Calidris temminckii* 14 cm 5½ in. Nests among low plants in far north, and winters in Africa. During migration in spring and autumn may be seen throughout Europe (though unlikely in British Isles), mainly in marshes.

Dunlin *Calidris alpina* 18 cm 7 in. Nests on moors and in marshes;

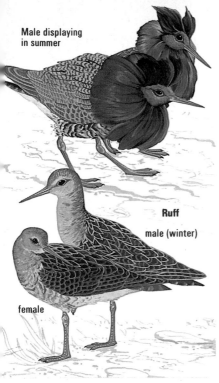

Male displaying in summer

Ruff

male (winter)

female

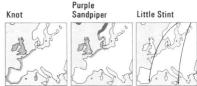

Knot | Purple Sandpiper | Little Stint

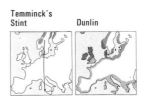

Temminck's Stint | Dunlin

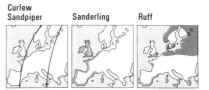

Curlew Sandpiper | Sanderling | Ruff

spends winter in flocks on mudflats at or near coast and also inland. Flies in tight groups known as 'wader smoke' from the way the birds twist and turn through the air.

Curlew Sandpiper *Calidris ferruginea* 19 cm 7½ in. Nests in Arctic and winters to south of Europe. During migration in spring and autumn may be seen throughout Europe at mudflats and in marshes.

Sanderling *Calidris alba* 20 cm 8 in. Seen in winter at sandy beaches, racing about as if chasing the waves. Migrates to Arctic to breed.

Ruff *Philomachus pugnax* Male: 30 cm 12 in; female: 23 cm 9 in. Nests on moors and in marshes and meadows; also found beside rivers and lakes in winter. In late spring and early summer, the males attract the females by raising a beautiful ruff of feathers around the neck. The colour of the ruff varies greatly. The female is also known as a reeve.

Avocet

female

male
(winter)

male
(summer)

Black-winged Stilt

male
(summer)

winter

female
(summer)

**Red-necked
Phalarope**

AVOCETS AND STILTS

Family Recurvirostridae

These birds are the most elegant wading birds. They pick their way through the shallow water on stilt-like legs, snapping up insects from the air or lowering their long thin beaks into the water.

Avocet *Recurvirostra avosetta* 43 cm 17 in. Nests in marshes at or near coast; spends winter at estuaries. Best seen at bird reserves. Beak curves upwards so that the end skims surface of water.
Black–winged Stilt *Himantopus himantopus* 38 cm 15 in. Found in marshes and lagoons, often wading deeply in large stretches of water.

PHALAROPES

Family Phalaropodidae

Red–necked Phalarope *Phalaropus lobatus* 18 cm 7 in. Nests in marshes and beside lakes; spends winter out to sea. Often swims, unlike other waders, floating high in the water and sometimes spinning in circles to stir up small animals from the bottom. Phalaropes are unusual birds. The females court the males, and the males build the nest, sit on the eggs and raise the young.

THICK-KNEES

Family Burhinidae

Stone Curlew *Burhinus oedicnemus* 41 cm 16 in. Gets its name because it is often found in stony and rocky places, and because its call (usually heard after dark) is like that of a curlew. Also found in open treeless country. Runs with its head down when disturbed. Thick-knees got their strange name because their 'knees' (which are in fact their heels) appear to be swollen.

Stone Curlew

PRATINCOLES

Family Glareolidae

Pratincole *Glareola pratincola* 25 cm 10 in. Found on dried mudflats and grassy plains, and at open spaces in marshes. Pratincoles fly and look like large swallows, but also run about the ground. They often stand on tiptoe and stretch their necks, as if trying to see something.

SKUAS

Family Stercorariidae

Skuas are sea birds, as are gulls, terns and auks. They are also pirates of the skies, for they often chase other sea birds and make them drop a fish they have just captured or even half eaten! The skua then swoops down to catch its stolen meal before it hits the water below.

Great Skua *Stercorarius skua* 58 cm 23 in. Nests among grass or heather on moors, and spends winter out to sea. May be seen at coast on migration in spring and autumn.
Arctic Skua *Stercorarius parasiticus* 46 cm 18 in. Lives in similar places to great skua. The neck, breast and underparts may be light, dark or any shade between.

Pratincole

Great Skua diving

Great Skua

dark form

light form

Arctic Skua

Avocet

Black-winged Stilt

Red-necked Phalarope

Stone Curlew

Pratincole

Great Skua

Arctic Skua

61

GULLS AND TERNS

Family Laridae

These two kinds of sea birds are easy to tell apart. Gulls have broad wings and fan-shaped tails, and their beaks are usually heavy with a hooked tip. They can be seen in flocks at the seashore and at harbours, constantly making mewing cries as they wheel to and fro in the air. To feed, they settle on the water and seize some floating waste or dip their heads under the water to catch a fish. They also follow ships, but not out of sight of land. Gulls also fly inland, especially in winter. They can be seen looking for scraps of food on rubbish tips and in parks, and chasing ploughs as they turn the soil in the fields. They nest in colonies on the ground and on cliffs. Young gulls look brown and white until they are as much as four years old.

Terns (see pages 66 and 67) have slender wings and forked tails, and sharp beaks that often point downwards during flight. They fly low and sometimes hover over the water, and then dive to catch fish. Terns can be seen at the seashore and at inland marshes and lakes. They nest on the ground in colonies, and may attack any person or animal approaching too close to the nest. Terns migrate great distances to spend the winter far to the south.

A flock of gulls. These birds often follow ploughs to pick up worms and grubs as the soil is turned over. The gulls are helpful to farmers because they devour pests in this way.

Great Black-backed Gull

Lesser Black-backed Gull

Herring Gull

Common Gull

Glaucous Gull

62

Great Black-backed Gull

British form

Scandinavian form

Lesser Black-backed Gull

Great Black–backed Gull *Larus marinus* 68 cm 27 in. Usually seen at rocky coasts and offshore islands; may be seen inland, especially in winter. Often feeds on eggs and young of other sea birds.

Lesser Black–backed Gull *Larus fuscus* 53 cm 21 in. Often seen at seashore and harbours and also inland. The British form (*Larus fuscus graellsii*) has a lighter back than the Scandinavian form (*Larus fuscus fuscus*), which looks like a small great black-backed gull.

Herring Gull *Larus argentatus* 56 cm 22 in. A very common gull, seen both at the coast and inland.

Common Gull *Larus canus* 41 cm 16 in. Found at coast and inland. In spite of its name, it is not the most numerous gull.

Glaucous Gull *Larus hyperboreus* 71 cm 28 in. Nests in Iceland and in Arctic; seen at coasts and harbours in winter, rarely inland. Preys on eggs and small birds.

WHAT TO LOOK FOR

Great Black-backed Gull Black back and wings, pink legs.

Lesser Black-backed Gull Dark grey back and wings (British form) or black back and wings (Scandinavian form); legs usually yellow or orange.

Herring Gull Pale grey back and wings with black and white wingtips and red spot on yellow bill; legs usually pink.

Common Gull As herring gull, but yellow-green legs and greenish bill without red spot.

Glaucous Gull Silver-grey back and wings; no dark patches at wingtips.

Herring Gull

Glaucous Gull

Common Gull

Mediterranean Gull
summer

Slender-billed Gull

Little Gull
summer

Mediterranean
Gull in winter

Little Gull
in winter

Slender–billed Gull *Larus genei* 43 cm 17 in. Nests in marshes and by lagoons and rivers, but is otherwise found at coasts and river mouths. Long bill is pointed down in flight.

Mediterranean Gull *Larus melanocephalus* 38 cm 15 in. Nests in marshes and by lakes and lagoons, otherwise seen at seashore and harbours and also inland.

Little Gull *Larus minutus* 28 cm 11 in. Gets its name because it is noticeably smaller than other gulls. Nests in marshes and swamps, but seen at coast and inland at other times. Catches insects in flight.

Black–headed Gull *Larus ridibundus* 38 cm 15 in. A very common gull, often seen inland. Nests in marshes, on moors, and by lakes and rivers. At other times found at coasts and harbours, and in fields and towns. Eats anything, including fish, worms, flying insects and even garbage. Badly named, as other gulls have black heads and the head is dark brown but goes white in winter !

Sabine's Gull *Larus sabini* 33 cm 13 in. Nests in Arctic, and spends winter out to sea but may be seen at coast. Only European gull with noticeably forked tail.

Kittiwake *Rissa tridactyla* 41 cm 16 in. Nests in colonies on cliff ledges and also on buildings in coastal towns. Usually spends winter far out to sea.

WHAT TO LOOK FOR

Slender-billed Gull As black-headed gull but white head throughout year and long thin bill.

Mediterranean Gull As black-headed gull but black head in summer, and no black edge on back of wings.

Little Gull Like small black-headed gull but black head in summer, no black on wingtips and dark beneath wings.

Black-headed Gull Dark-brown head (summer only); white patch on front of wings and black edge on back of wings.

Sabine's Gull As black-headed gull, but dark-grey head in summer, black wingtips and forked tail.

Kittiwake Solid black wingtips and black legs.

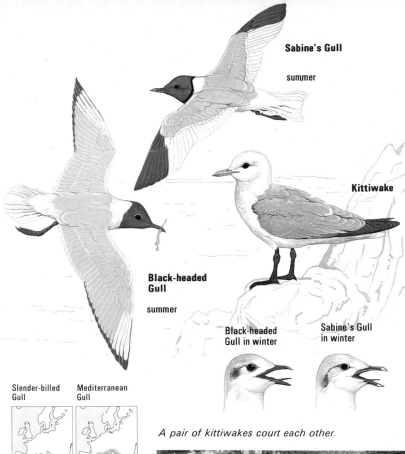

Sabine's Gull

summer

Kittiwake

Black-headed Gull

summer

Black-headed Gull in winter

Sabine's Gull in winter

Slender-billed Gull

Mediterranean Gull

Little Gull

Black-headed Gull

Sabine's Gull

Kittiwake

A pair of kittiwakes court each other.

65

Black Tern

Common Tern

Whiskered Tern

Arctic Tern

Black Tern *Chlidonias niger* 24 cm 9½ in. Builds floating nest on lakes and marsh pools; may be seen at coast during migration in spring and autumn. Chases insects in air; rarely dives into water.

Whiskered Tern *Chlidonias hybrida* 24 cm 9½ in. Found in same places as black tern, but often dives for food.

Common Tern *Sterna hirundo* 36 cm 14 in. Nests on beaches, among sand dunes, in coastal swamps, on offshore islands and by lakes. Often seen flying along seashore and diving for fish.

Arctic Tern *Sterna paradisaea* 36 cm 14 in. Found in same kinds of places as common tern, but less likely inland. May migrate as far south as the Antarctic to spend the winter.

Roseate Tern *Sterna dougallii* 38 cm 15 in. Nests on rocky islands and beaches, sometimes with common terns and arctic terns; seldom found inland.

Little Tern *Sterna albifrons* 24 cm 9½ in. Nests mainly on sandy and stony beaches, but sometimes at places inland.

Sandwich Tern *Sterna sandvicensis* 41 cm 16 in. Nests in colonies on sandy and stony beaches and also on offshore islands. Rarely found inland. Named after Sandwich in Kent, where a famous colony once existed.

WHAT TO LOOK FOR
Black Tern Black head and body, grey wings and tail.
Whiskered Tern Grey belly, white cheeks.
Common Tern Orange bill, black tip.
Arctic Tern All-red bill; short legs.
Roseate Tern All-black bill, sometimes with red base; very long tail.
Little Tern Yellow bill with black tip, white forehead.
Sandwich Tern Black bill with yellow tip; slight crest.

NOTE: the descriptions and illustrations on these pages are of birds in summer plumage. Terns may also be seen in winter plumage, when they all have white foreheads and dark bills, and are very difficult to tell apart. In addition, the black tern and whiskered tern become white beneath.

The nest of this arctic tern is a shallow hole scraped in a stony beach.

Black Tern   **Whiskered Tern**   **Common Tern**   **Arctic Tern**

Roseate Tern   **Little Tern**   **Sandwich Tern**

Sandwich Tern

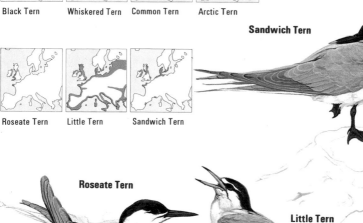

Roseate Tern

Little Tern

67

AUKS

Family Alcidae

Auks look and behave very much like penguins. They dive for fish and chase them underwater, using their wings like oars and their feet like a rudder. On land, they sit up and waddle about. Also like penguins, they spend most of the year at sea and only come ashore to breed. However, unlike penguins, they can fly well – although the great auk, which is now extinct, could not. It was a very easy target for hunters, and the last pair of birds was killed in 1844. The great auk was a large bird as big as a goose. The little auk is much smaller and still survives and breeds in Arctic regions.

A puffin (right). The beak has saw-tooth edges so that the puffin can hold several fish in its beak at once. Puffins are most likely to be seen in spring and summer when they nest in burrows dug into soil at cliffs by the sea. The oddly-shaped beak is very colourful at this time.

Razorbill

Little Auk

Guillemot

Black
Guillemot

Puffin

Razorbill

summer

winter

summer

winter

Little Auk

summer

winter

Puffin

Razorbill *Alca torda* 41 cm 16 in. Breeds in colonies on cliff ledges at coast, often with guillemots. Spends winter out to sea, although storms may force it back to shore.

Little Auk *Plautus alle* 20 cm 8 in. Nests in Arctic and spends winter in northern seas, but may be driven ashore by storms.

Puffin *Fratercula arctica* 30 cm 12 in. Nests in colonies in burrows in steep slopes by sea. May run down slope to get into the air. Can hold several fish at once in its parrot-like beak. Spends winter far out to sea and seldom blown ashore.

Black Guillemot *Cepphus grylle* 33 cm 13 in. Nests in holes and crevices on rocky shores and sea cliffs, but not in large colonies. Stays near shore in winter.

Guillemot *Uria aalge* 41 cm 16 in. Breeds in large colonies on cliff ledges at coast and on offshore islands. The guillemot's egg is laid on bare rock and is pear-shaped, so that it rolls in a circle and not over the edge if knocked. Spends winter out to sea, but may be driven ashore by gales.

WHAT TO LOOK FOR

Razorbill Broad dark bill with white marks.

Little Auk Small size and short bill.

Puffin Triangular beak (bright red and yellow in summer).

Black Guillemot Summer: black body with white wing patch. Winter: mottled grey back with white wing patch.

Guillemot Slender pointed bill.

Guillemot

summer

winter

summer

winter

Black Guillemot

female

male

Pallas's Sandgrouse

Stock Dove

Rock Dove

PIGEONS AND DOVES

Order Columbiformes

These birds have plump bodies, small heads and short legs. They can all fly very fast, and people raise pigeons for racing. There are two families, sandgrouse (family Pteroclidae) and pigeons and doves (family Columbidae). Sandgrouse live and nest on dry sandy or stony ground, and may have to fly long distances to find water. Only one species, Pallas's sandgrouse, is likely to be seen throughout Europe. Pigeons and doves are also likely to be seen waddling about on the ground, pecking for food. They can suck up water to drink, unlike other birds which have to tip their heads back to get the water to flow down their throats. Pigeons and doves nest in trees or holes or on cliff ledges. There is no particular difference between pigeons and doves.

WHAT TO LOOK FOR

Pallas's Sandgrouse Dark patch on belly, long pointed tail.

Stock Dove Grey rump, no obvious neck mark or wing marks.

Rock Dove White rump, no neck mark, two black wing stripes.

Woodpigeon Grey rump, white neck mark, white wingbar.

Turtle Dove Black tail with white edges; white neck patch with black stripes.

Collared Dove Black stripe edged with white at back of neck.

Pallas's Sandgrouse

Stock Dove

Rock Dove

Pallas's Sandgrouse *Syrrhaptes paradoxus* 38 cm 15 in. Nests in central Asia, and sometimes migrates to Europe. Likely to be seen at sandy shores and in fields after the harvesting season

Stock Dove *Columba oenas* 33 cm 13 in. Found in woods and on farmland; may also be seen in parks and at cliffs and sand dunes along coast. Often found in the company of woodpigeons.

Rock Dove *Columba livia* 33 cm 13 in. Lives at rocky coasts and on mountains, and nests in caves and on cliff ledges. The pigeons that can be seen in city squares and parks, as well as the pigeons that people raise for racing, are all descended from the wild rock dove. Some of these pigeons still look like their wild ancestor, but many now have different plumage. The pigeons are interbreeding with the rock doves, and the wild birds are slowly disappearing.

   Because the wild birds are naturally at home on cliffs, pigeons can live and nest on the ledges of buildings. They have long been a companion of man, carrying messages for him as well as providing him with a source of food.

Woodpigeon *Columba palumbus* 41 cm 16 in. Found in woods and on farmland, and also in parks and gardens. Often seen in flocks containing stock doves and domestic pigeons.

Turtle Dove *Streptopelia turtur* 28 cm 11 in. Found in spring and summer in light woods and among scattered trees and bushes; also on farmland and in parks and gardens.

Collared Dove *Streptopelia decaocto* 30 cm 12 in. Usually found in towns or close to houses and farms. Nests on buildings or in trees nearby. Until 1930, collared doves lived in Asia and south-east Europe. Then they began to spread to the north-west. They reached Britain in 1955 and have recently moved on to Iceland. No-one knows why this has happened. Perhaps the collared doves have moved in because people have stopped raising pigeons in dovecots, or perhaps changes in farming have enabled them to spread.

Woodpigeon

Collared Dove

Turtle Dove

Woodpigeon	Turtle Dove	Collared Dove

Cuckoo

grey
form
(adult)

red
form
(young)

**Great Spotted
Cuckoo**

CUCKOOS

Order Cuculiformes Family Cuculidae

Cuckoos are famous for laying their eggs in the nests of other birds and leaving the other birds to bring up the young cuckoos. Both of the cuckoos found in Europe breed in this way. Cuckoos get their name from the unmistakable call that heralds their arrival in spring. In fact, this call is made by the male of only one species.

Cuckoo *Cuculus canorus* 33 cm 13 in. Found in woodland, open ground with scattered trees and bushes, and on moors. Only the male makes 'cuckoo' call; female has babbling call. The female cuckoo lays several eggs, one each in the nests of other birds. Small birds are chosen, such as meadow pipits and robins, but each female cuckoo always uses nests of the same species. When it hatches, the young cuckoo pushes out any other eggs and nestlings, but its adopted parents continue to feed it, driven by instinct.
Great Spotted Cuckoo *Clamator glandarius* 41 cm 16 in. Found in woods and among scattered trees. Does not call 'cuckoo'. Usually lays its eggs in the nests of crows, particularly magpies.

Cuckoo

Great Spotted
Cuckoo

Barn Owl

Scops Owl

Eagle Owl

Snowy Owl

WHAT TO LOOK FOR

Cuckoo Grey head and breast with bars on white underside; but female sometimes red-brown with bars all over body.

Great Spotted Cuckoo White spots on wings, grey crest, long white-edged tail.

Barn Owl Heart-shaped face; brown back with white or buff unstreaked breast (may look all white at dusk.)

Scops Owl Small, with short ear tufts.

Eagle Owl Huge, with long ear tufts.

Snowy Owl White plumage, large yellow eyes.

OWLS
Order Strigiformes

Owls are not often seen because they usually come out only at night to hunt mice and other small animals. However, their unusual hoot gives a clue to their whereabouts, and in the daytime small birds may gather around a sleeping owl and try to make it fly away. Owls have large eyes set in front of their heads to help them spot their prey in the dark. They also fly without a sound. Owls nest in holes in trees or the ground, or sometimes in buildings. There are two groups: barn owls (family Tytonidae) and all other owls (family Strigidae).

Barn Owl *Tyto alba* 36 cm 14 in. Found on farmland and in marshes but also occupies unused buildings, such as barns and church towers, and ruins. Most likely to be seen at dusk. Two forms occur, a white-breasted form (*Tyto alba alba*) in south and west Europe, and a buff-breasted form (*Tyto alba guttata*) in north and east Europe.

Scops Owl *Otus scops* 19 cm 7½ in. Found among trees, often near buildings, as well as in ruins. Rarely seen in daytime. Like other owls, has ear tufts that are not ears but merely tufts of head feathers.

Eagle Owl *Bubo bubo* 68 cm 27 in. Largest European owl. Lives in forests, among mountain crags and gorges, and on dry plains. Active at dawn and dusk, when it hunts animals as large as hares. Rare.

Snowy Owl *Nyctea scandiaca* 61 cm 24 in. Lives and nests in Arctic, Norway and Iceland, but sometimes spreads to northern Europe for the winter. May then be seen on moors, in marshes and at lake shores and coast. Hunts by day, but white plumage may conceal it against snow.

dark-breasted form

Barn Owl

light-breasted form

Scops Owl

Eagle Owl

Snowy Owl

Pygmy Owl

Little Owl

brown form

Tawny Owl

grey form

Pygmy Owl *Glaucidium passerinum* 18 cm 7 in. Usually seen in fir forests. Active day and night, chasing small birds through air. Flicks tail up and down when perching. Smallest European owl.

Little Owl *Athene noctua* 23 cm 9 in. Found among scattered trees, in fields and on open ground, often near buildings. May be seen in daytime, bobbing and turning its head as it perches on a post or branch.

Tawny Owl *Strix aluco* 38 cm 15 in. A very common owl. Lives in woods and also in parks and gardens. Usually hunts by night, but may be seen sleeping in tree during daytime, when it is sometimes bothered by small birds. Colour varies from brown to grey.

Long–eared Owl *Asio otus* 36 cm 14 in. Sleeps in woods, especially in fir trees, by day and comes out to hunt, often over open ground, at dusk. May be seen sleeping in groups in winter.

Short–eared Owl *Asio flammeus* 38 cm 15 in. Seen hunting over moors, marshes and open ground during daytime and at dusk. Ear tufts are very short, often invisible.

Tengmalm's Owl *Aegolius funereus* 25 cm 10 in. Usually found in fir forests; active at night.

Long-eared Owl

Short-eared Owl

Tengmalm's Owl

A nightjar nesting.

NIGHTJARS

Order Caprimulgiformes
Family Caprimulgidae

Nightjar *Caprimulgus europaeu.* 28 cm 11 in. Lives in woods, among bracken in clearings and on hillsides, on moors and in sand dunes. Unless disturbed, it is very difficult to spot. Sleeps during the day and hunts for insects at night. Lays eggs on the ground.

male

female

Pygmy Owl

Nightjar

WHAT TO LOOK FOR

Pygmy Owl Very small, with round head, no ear tufts; flicks tail when sitting on perch.

Little Owl Small, with flattened head, no ear tufts.

Tawny Owl Streaky plumage with black eyes; stocky shape and no ear tufts.

Long-eared Owl Slender shape and long ear tufts.

Short-eared Owl Similar to tawny owl but yellow eyes and lighter plumage.

Tengmalm's Owl Like little owl but rounder head and prominent eyebrows.

Nightjar Plumage pattern looks like dead leaves from above; fine bars below.

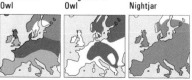

Little Owl   Tawny Owl   Long-eared Owl

Short-eared Owl   Tengmalm's Owl   Nightjar

Swift

SWIFTS

Order Apodiformes Family Apodidae

Swifts are masters of the air and are usually seen in flocks, wheeling high in the sky at great speed. They may spend weeks in the air without coming down, as they catch flying insects for food and can sleep in flight. Swifts have weak feet and if they land on the ground, they cannot walk and find it hard to get back into the air. Instead, they usually cling to vertical surfaces and simply fall off them to become airborne.

WHAT TO LOOK FOR

Swift Dark body; shallow forked tail.

Alpine Swift White belly and throat with dark breast band; very long wings.

Kingfisher Blue-green back and orange underparts.

Bee-eater Yellow throat and blue-green breast.

Roller Blue-green with chestnut back.

Hoopoe Black-and-white striped wings; large black-tipped crest.

Swift *Apus apus* 16 cm 6½ in. Nests in holes in trees, crevices in cliffs, and under the eaves of buildings. Often to be seen at dusk, dashing around rooftops in noisy flocks. May be seen with swallows (page 84), but can easily be recognized by dark underparts and shallow forked tail.

Alpine Swift *Apus melba* 20 cm 8 in. Found in mountains, at cliffs and around buildings. Nests in crevices. Has very long wings, unlike similar sand martin (picture, page 85).

Swift

Alpine Swift

Kingfisher

Bee-eater

Roller

Hoopoe

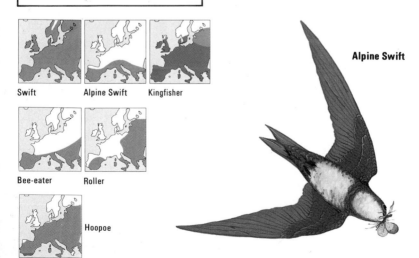

Alpine Swift

KINGFISHERS AND RELATED BIRDS

Order Coraciiformes

Any birds in this mixed group are worth a special effort to see, for they are the most colourful and spectacular birds to be seen in Europe. None is like any other and they all belong to different families. The kingfisher belongs to the family Alcedinidae, and the bee-eater to the family Meropidae. The roller is a member of the family Coraciidae, and the hoopoe of the family Upupidae.

Kingfisher

Kingfisher *Alcedo atthis* 16 cm 6½ in. Seen by rivers and lakes, perching on a branch beside the water or darting down to plunge for a fish. May also be seen at coast in winter.

Bee-eater *Merops apiaster* 28 cm 11 in. Found in open country among scattered trees and bushes, often perching on bushes or telegraph wires. Nests in hole dug in bank of river or pit, or in burrow dug in the ground. Chases flying insects, especially bees and wasps.

Roller *Coracias garrulus* 30 cm 12 in. Found in open country with scattered trees and in woods. Nests in hole in tree or bank. Often seen perching and then swooping down to catch insects and other small animals. Gets its name from the way it rolls over in flight to attract a mate during the spring courtship.

Hoopoe *Upupa epops* 28 cm 11 in. Seen among scattered trees and in woods; sometimes in parks and gardens. Nests in hole in tree or wall. Often seen perching, usually with its crest down. Named after its call.

Bee-eater

Roller

crest up

Hoopoe

crest down

WOODPECKERS

Order Piciformes Family Picidae

Woodpeckers are often heard before being seen. Their sharp beaks make a loud rat-a-tat as they chisel into the bark of a tree in search of insects. They also dig out holes for nesting. Woodpeckers grip the trunk or branch with sharp claws and thrust their tails stiffly against the bark to prop themselves up and give a powerful blow with the beak. In the spring, they make a drumming noise by clattering their beaks on a piece of wood; this is part of their courtship.

female

Three-toed Woodpecker

male

foot

Wryneck

Green Woodpecker *Picus viridis* 30 cm 12 in. Found in woods and forests, usually of broad-leaved trees, and in open country with scattered trees. Also seen on ground, feeding at anthills.

Grey-headed Woodpecker *Picus canus* 25 cm 10 in. Found in same places as green woodpecker. Often drums in spring, unlike green woodpecker.

Three-toed Woodpecker *Picoides tridactylus* 23 cm 9 in. Lives in forests on mountains and in far north.

Black Woodpecker *Dryocopus martius* 46 cm 18 in. Lives in woods and forests, often in mountains. Largest European woodpecker.

Wryneck *Jynx torquilla* 16 cm 6½ in. Lives in light woodland, and in open country with scattered trees, bushes and hedges, orchards, parks and gardens. Does not look like a woodpecker and does not chisel into bark. Often feeds on ground and nests in existing holes, including nest-boxes. Gets its name from the way it can turn its head round.

WHAT TO LOOK FOR

Green Woodpecker Greenish back and yellow rump; large red crown. Thick black (female) or red (male) moustache.

Grey-headed Woodpecker Grey head with thin moustache; male only has red forehead.

Three-toed Woodpecker White back, black cheeks and striped flanks. Yellow crown (male only).

Black Woodpecker Black body with red crown.

Wryneck Long banded tail; small beak.

Green Woodpecker

Grey-headed Woodpecker

Three-toed Woodpecker

Black Woodpecker

Wryneck

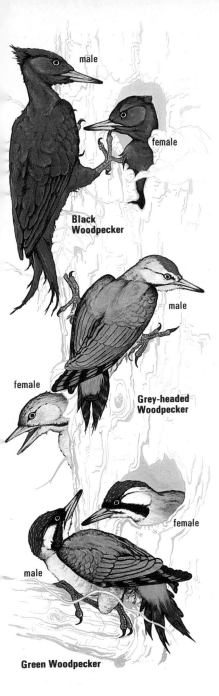

male

female

Black Woodpecker

male

female

Grey-headed Woodpecker

female

male

Green Woodpecker

A female great spotted wood-pecker feeding its young.
It lays up to eight white eggs in the hole it chisels out of a tree trunk or branch. While feeding its young at the entrance hole to the nest, the adult bird clings to the tree with its powerful claws and props itself up by its stiff tail.

Syrian Woodpecker *Dendrocopos syriacus* 23 cm 9 in. Found in woods and forests, and also around villages and farms.

Great Spotted Woodpecker *Dendrocopos major* 23 cm 9 in. Found in woods and forests of all kinds, and also in parks and gardens. Comes to bird tables.

Middle Spotted Woodpecker *Dendrocopos medius* 20 cm 8 in. Lives in woods and forests, though seldom among fir trees. Usually stays high up in trees.

Lesser Spotted Woodpecker *Dendrocopos minor* 15 cm 6 in. Lives in same places as middle spotted woodpecker, but may also be found in parks and orchards. Smallest European woodpecker.

White–backed Woodpecker *Dendrocopos leucotos* 25 cm 10 in. Found in woods and forests, though not often among fir trees.

male

female

Syrian Woodpecker

A wryneck with its crest displayed

WHAT TO LOOK FOR

Syrian Woodpecker As great spotted woodpecker, but no black neck stripe.

Great Spotted Woodpecker Large white wing patch and black crown (red in young); black stripe across neck; red patch at back of head (male only).

Middle Spotted Woodpecker As great spotted woodpecker, but red crown in both sexes and less black on face.

Lesser Spotted Woodpecker Small; black and white stripes on back with no red under tail. Crown red (male) or whitish (female).

White-backed Woodpecker As lesser spotted woodpecker, but larger and with white rump and red under tail.

Syrian Woodpecker	Great Spotted Woodpecker	Middle Spotted Woodpecker	Lesser Spotted Woodpecker	White-backed Woodpecker

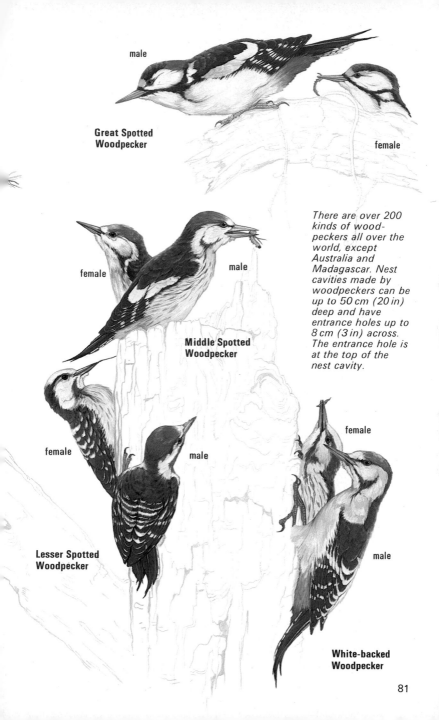

male

Great Spotted Woodpecker

female

female

male

Middle Spotted Woodpecker

There are over 200 kinds of wood-peckers all over the world, except Australia and Madagascar. Nest cavities made by woodpeckers can be up to 50 cm (20 in) deep and have entrance holes up to 8 cm (3 in) across. The entrance hole is at the top of the nest cavity.

female

female

male

Lesser Spotted Woodpecker

male

White-backed Woodpecker

81

Short-toed Lark

Calandra Lark

Crested Lark

PERCHING BIRDS AND SONGBIRDS
Order Passeriformes

These birds make up the biggest group of birds – more than half of all birds. They are to be found everywhere. None is very large, and most are fairly small. Their feet have three toes in front and a long one behind, which enables them to perch easily – although, of course, other birds can perch too. Many, but by no means all, can sing well and, in a few cases, the song must be heard to be sure of the bird's identity.

A skylark at its nest.

LARKS
Family Alaudidae

These birds are most often seen in the air, singing strongly. They make their nests on the ground where, being dull-coloured, they are difficult to spot. However, they may sometimes be seen running along the ground. Some larks look rather like buntings (pages 122-124), but have thin beaks whereas buntings have stout beaks.

Skylark

Woodlark

Shore Lark

Calandra Lark

Short-toed Lark

Crested Lark

Woodlark

Skylark

Shore Lark

WHAT TO LOOK FOR

Calandra Lark Black neck patch and large beak.

Short-toed Lark Pale unstreaked underside.

Crested Lark Large crest (Note: in southern Spain, almost identical Thekla lark – Galerida theklae – may be seen).

Woodlark Black and white mark at front of wing; all-brown tail; slight crest.

Skylark White edges to tail; slight crest.

Shore Lark Horns on head (male only); black and yellow face pattern.

Calandra Lark *Melanocorypha calandra* 19 cm 7½ in. Found on stony ground and plains and in fields.

Short–toed Lark *Calandrella cinerea* 14 cm 5½ in. Lives on dry, bare sandy or stony ground, dried mudflats and plains and in fields.

Crested Lark *Galerida cristata* 16 cm 6½ in. Found on stony and sandy ground and in fields; also seen on waste land in towns and villages and beside roads.

Woodlark *Lullula arborea* 15 cm 6 in. Found in fields and open country,

often among scattered trees and bushes, and at woodland edges. Often flies in circle while singing; also sings while perched.

Skylark *Alauda arvensis* 18 cm 7 in. Found in all kinds of open country – moors, marshes, fields and sand dunes. Rises straight up into air and may hover while singing.

Shore Lark *Eremophila alpestris* 16 cm 6½ in. Nests on rocky ground in far north or high in mountains. Spends winter at beaches, and in marshes and fields along coast.

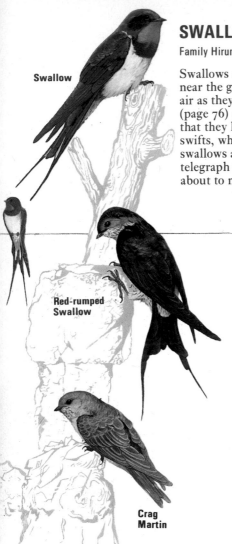

Swallow

Red-rumped Swallow

Crag Martin

SWALLOWS AND MARTINS

Family Hirundinidae

Swallows and martins fly very fast, often near the ground, twisting and turning in the air as they chase flying insects. Swifts (page 76) are similar, but have longer wings that they hold out stiffly as they fly. Unlike swifts, which cannot perch, flocks of swallows and martins often perch on telegraph wires, especially when they are about to migrate.

Swallow *Hirundo rustica* 19 cm 7½ in. Builds an open nest of mud and straw on beams and ledges in farm buildings and sheds. Hunts for insects in nearby fields, often swooping low in flight over water.

Red–rumped Swallow *Hirundo daurica* 18 cm 7 in. Usually found in rocky country and at coast. Builds mud nest with long narrow entrance on walls of caves, cliffs or rocks, under bridges, or on buildings.

Crag Martin *Hirundo rupestris* 14 cm 5½ in. Lives in mountains and on sea cliffs. Builds cup-shaped mud nest on rock face or cave wall, and sometimes on buildings.

House Martin *Delichon urbica* 13 cm 5 in. Often seen in towns and villages, but also lives in open country. Builds mud nest with tiny entrance hole beneath eaves of buildings, under bridges, and also on rock faces and cliffs.

Sand Martin *Riparia riparia* 13 cm 5 in. Lives in open country, especially near ponds, lakes and rivers. Nests in colonies in holes dug in banks of rivers, cuttings and pits, and also in cliffs.

Swallow	Red-rumped Swallow	Crag Martin	House Martin	Sand Martin	Golden Oriole

Sand Martin

female

male

House Martin

Golden Oriole

ORIOLES

Family Oriolidae

Most orioles are brightly coloured birds of tropical forests. Only one species is found as far north as Europe.

Golden Oriole *Oriolus oriolus* 24 cm 9½ in. Found in woods and orchards, and among trees in parks. Usually hides among leaves in tree tops.

WHAT TO LOOK FOR

Swallow Deeply forked tail, red throat, deep blue back.

Red-rumped Swallow As swallow but without red throat and with buff (not red) rump.

Crag Martin Brown back and underside completely pale buff.

House Martin Deep blue back with white rump, underside completely white.

Sand Martin As crag martin but brown breast band.

Golden Oriole Male: bright yellow with black wings. Female: head and body green above and streaky white below.

House martins gather in large numbers along telegraph wires in European countries in the autumn as they get ready to migrate to Africa for the winter.

CROWS

Family Corvidae

Crows are the largest perching birds and they are among the cleverest of all birds. They search boldly for all kinds of food, and will avoid traps and ignore scarecrows that farmers put out to stop them robbing crops. They may also store food for the winter, and open snails by dropping them on to a stone. Crows caw and screech rather than sing.

A rookery. Rooks build their untidy nests high in the tree tops for safety. They build their nests in such large colonies because they are sociable birds. Jackdaws and owls may sometimes take over nests that have been abandoned by rooks.

Raven *Corvus corax* 63 cm 25 in. Lives on sea cliffs and crags, in woods and open country, especially in hills and mountains and usually far from towns and villages. Builds huge nest on rock ledge or in tree. Often makes acrobatic display in the air, especially in spring. Hunts animals such as rabbits, hedgehogs and rats, but usually eats dead animals. The largest all-black bird found in Europe.

Raven

Carrion Crow

Hooded Crow

Jackdaw

Rook

Carrion Crow *Corvus corone corone*
46 cm 18 in. Found on moors, at
coasts and in fields, parks and gardens.
Often seen alone or in pairs, and pairs
nest alone in trees or on cliffs. Usually
simply called crow rather than carrion
crow.

Hooded Crow *Corvus corone cornix*
46 cm 18 in. Found in same places and
lives in same way as carrion crow.
Belongs to same species as carrion
crow, and interbreeds with it in places
where their ranges overlap, producing
birds intermediate in appearance
between them.

Rook *Corvus frugilegus* 46 cm 18 in.
Found in fields surrounded by lines of
trees or small woods, in which it nests
in colonies called rookeries. Also at
seashore and open ground in winter.
Usually seen in groups, often by
motorways.

Jackdaw *Corvus monedula* 33 cm
13 in. Found in fields and open country
and at rocky coasts, nesting in holes
in trees and rocks. Also seen on
farms, and in towns and villages,
where it nests in old buildings. Usually
seen in flocks, walking jerkily or flying
acrobatically.

WHAT TO LOOK FOR

Raven Huge; all-black body with
massive black beak and wedge-shaped
tail.

Carrion Crow Medium size; all-black
body with heavy black beak.

Hooded Crow Like carrion crow but
grey back and belly.

Rook Like carrion crow, but grey patch
at base of beak (making beak look large).

Jackdaw Black body but back of head
and neck is grey.

Raven
Carrion Crow
Hooded Crow
Rook
Jackdaw

Magpie **Nutcracker**

An Alpine chough. This bird follows mountaineers and may be seen at the top of the highest mountains, particularly in the Alps and Pyrenees and the mountains of the Balkans. The alpine chough is a strong flier and can be seen soaring high in the sky in these areas.

Jay **Chough** **Alpine Chough**

Magpie **Nutcracker**

Magpie *Pica pica* 46 cm 18 in. Found in fields and open country with scattered trees and bushes, in which it builds a large dome-shaped nest. Often seen in town parks and gardens. May steal bright objects, and store them in its nest. It has a characteristic pattern of flight, in which it intermittently glides and then rapidly flaps its wings.

Nutcracker *Nucifraga caryocatactes* 33 cm 13 in. Lives in mountain forests, usually among conifer trees. Feeds mainly on nuts, which it may store in the autumn and find months later, even under snow.

Jay *Garrulus glandarius* 36 cm 14 in. Found in woods and orchards, and sometimes in town parks and gardens. Fond of acorns, which it stores for the winter by burying them in the ground. Can hold as many as six acorns in its mouth. It is a very lively and active bird and often flicks its tail. Its call is a harsh and noisy squawk.

Chough *Pyrrhocorax pyrrhocorax* 38 cm 15 in. Lives in mountains and on cliffs by sea; may also be found in quarries. Nests on ledges and in caves and crevices. Often performs aerobatics in flight.

Alpine Chough *Pyrrhocorax graculus* 38 cm 15 in. Lives on high mountains, right up to the snowy summits. Alpine choughs have even been seen near the top of Mount Everest, higher than any other bird. Comes down to mountain villages in winter to feed on any scraps it can find.

Jay

Chough

Alpine Chough

WHAT TO LOOK FOR

Magpie Black and white body with very long tail.

Nutcracker Brown body with white spots; white under tail.

Jay Blue and white patch on wing; white rump.

Chough Black body with red legs and red curved beak.

Alpine Chough As chough, but yellow beak.

TITS
Family Paridae

Great Tit

Blue Tit

Coal Tit

Tits are mainly woodland birds, but several kinds are frequent visitors to gardens. They can easily be told apart from other common woodland and garden birds as they have chunky rounded bodies. In woods, they flit through the branches and hang from twigs to get at insects, buds and seeds; they nest in holes in trees, laying at least four or five eggs and sometimes as many as twenty. Tits can easily be attracted to a garden; they are bold birds and show little fear of man. Their agility enables them to feed easily at bird tables and to take food hung from a branch or a gutter. Being hole nesters, they also come readily to nest boxes. Tits are most likely to be seen in flocks in autumn and winter.

A blue tit pecks through the lid of a milk bottle.

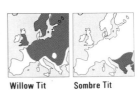

Willow Tit   Sombre Tit

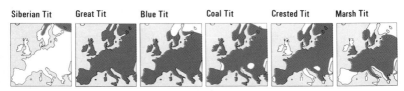

Siberian Tit   Great Tit   Blue Tit   Coal Tit   Crested Tit   Marsh Tit

Crested Tit

Willow Tit

Siberian Tit

Marsh Tit

Sombre Tit

WHAT TO LOOK FOR

Great Tit   Yellow breast with black central stripe.

Blue Tit   Blue cap, wings and tail.

Coal Tit   White patch at back of head.

Crested Tit   Speckled crest on head.

Marsh Tit   Black crown without white nape of coal tit.

Willow Tit   As marsh tit, but light wing patch.

Sombre Tit   As marsh tit, but large black patch on throat.

Siberian Tit   Brown crown, black throat.

Great Tit *Parus major* 14 cm 5½ in. Very often seen in woods, parks and gardens. Often pecks through milk bottle tops to reach the cream.
Blue Tit *Parus caeruleus* 11 cm 4½ in. Very often seen in woods, parks and gardens. Like great tit, it often opens milk bottles. Blue tits also tear strips from wallpaper, books and newspapers, an activity thought to be an extension of their habit of tearing bark from trees to find insects.
Coal Tit *Parus ater* 11 cm 4½ in. Common in woods, especially pine woods. Less often seen in gardens than great tit or blue tit.
Crested Tit *Parus cristatus* 11 cm 4½ in. Usually found in woods, especially among coniferous trees. Rarely seen in gardens.
Marsh Tit *Parus palustris* 11 cm 4½ in. Common in woods and often found in gardens. In spite of its name, it does not usually frequent marshes. Nests in natural holes in walls or trees.
Willow Tit *Parus montanus* 11 cm 4½ in. Common in woods, usually in damp places. Excavates nesting hole in rotten wood.
Sombre Tit *Parus lugubris* 14 cm 5½ in. Found in woods and rocky country. Less bold than other tits, and usually lives alone.
Siberian Tit *Parus cinctus* 13 cm 5 in. Found in woods. Has untidy plumage, unlike other tits.

LONG-TAILED TITS

Family Aegithalidae

Several families of birds are called tits, which is simply an old word meaning little. If it were not for their tails, which take up more than half their length, long-tailed tits would be among the world's tiniest birds. Only one species is found in Europe.

Long-tailed Tit *Aegithalos caudatus* 14 cm 5½ in. Found among bushes, thickets and hedges in woods, farmland and sometimes parks and gardens. Builds delicate globe-shaped nest with tiny entrance hole. The parent bird has to fold its long tail over its back when it is inside the nest.

PENDULINE TITS

Family Remizidae

Penduline means hanging, and these tits are named after their nests, which hang from a branch. Only one kind is seen in Europe.

Penduline Tit *Remiz pendulinus* 11 cm 4½ in. Found in marshes and along banks of rivers and lakes. Builds bag-like nest with funnel-shaped entrance among bushes or reeds.

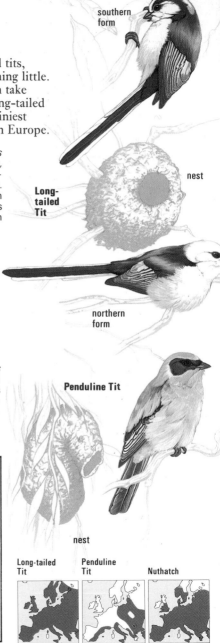

southern form

nest

Long-tailed Tit

northern form

Penduline Tit

nest

WHAT TO LOOK FOR

Long-tailed Tit Very small black and white body with very long tail.

Penduline Tit Brown and white with black patch around eye.

Nuthatch Blue-grey back, short tail.

Wallcreeper Crimson wing patch.

Treecreeper Curved beak; streaky brown back and all-white underside.

Short-toed Treecreeper Very similar to treecreeper, but may have buff flanks.

Long-tailed Tit   Penduline Tit   Nuthatch

Nuthatch

summer

winter

Wallcreeper

Treecreeper

Short-toed Treecreeper

NUTHATCHES AND WALLCREEPERS

Family Sittidae

Nuthatches are very agile tree birds, and are to be seen clambering up or running headfirst down trunks and along branches, picking insects from the bark.
Wallcreepers climb over rock faces as well as walls, looking more like treecreepers than nuthatches. They also flutter through the air like butterflies.

Nuthatch *Sitta europaea* 14 cm 5½ in. Lives in woods, parks and gardens; may visit bird tables. Nests in hole in tree, often plastering up entrance hole with mud. Two colour forms occur: birds with a white underside in northern Europe (*Sitta europaea europaea*), and birds with a buff underside elsewhere (*Sitta europaea caesia*). In Yugoslavia, Greece and Turkey, the very similar rock nuthatch (*Sitta neumayer*) may be seen climbing rock faces.
Wallcreeper *Tichodroma muraria* 16 cm 6½ in. Lives on mountain slopes, among gorges and cliffs; descends to valleys and foothills in winter, when it may be seen on buildings. Nests in rock cavities.

TREECREEPERS

Family Certhiidae

These birds are named after the way they creep up tree trunks, seeking insects in the bark. They nest in holes and crevices in trees and behind ivy.

Treecreeper *Certhia familiaris* 13 cm 5 in. Found in woods, parks and gardens. Often seen with tits in winter.
Short-toed Treecreeper *Certhia brachydactyla* 13 cm 5 in. Lives in same places as treecreeper. In central and southern Europe, this species is usually found at low altitude, whereas the treecreeper often prefers the mountains here.

Wallcreeper **Treecreeper** **Short-toed Treecreeper**

WRENS
Family Troglodytidae

All but one of the members of the wren family live in America. They are all very small birds.

Wren *Troglodytes troglodytes* 10 cm 4 in. Lives among low plants almost anywhere, from mountains, coasts and moors to woods, fields, parks and gardens. Often seen scurrying about in a flower bed or along the bottom of a hedge or wall, seeking insects among the litter on the ground. Nests in hedges and bushes and in holes in walls and trees.

DIPPERS
Family Cinclidae

Dippers are unusual perching birds because they are water birds. They can swim and dive, and may even walk along the bottom of a stream to look for small freshwater animals. They are called dippers not because they are continually taking a dip, but because they bob their heads up and down as they perch on an overhanging branch or rock. Only one species lives in Europe.

Dipper *Cinclus cinclus* 18 cm 7 in. Lives by streams in mountains; may also be found by water at lower levels and at seashore in winter. Builds nest in river banks, under bridges or behind waterfalls.

BABBLERS
Family Timaliidae

Babblers get their name from their constant chatter. Only one species is found in Europe.

Bearded Tit or **Reedling** *Panurus biarmicus* 16 cm 6½ in. Lives among reeds; seen in flocks during winter. Gets its name from the large moustache marking of the male bird.

THRUSHES

Family Turdidae

This large family of birds contains several birds that are well known as visitors to gardens. They feed mainly on fruits, berries and insects, but are often to be seen looking for worms. Thrushes have beautiful songs, which they seem to perform just for the pleasure of singing.

Mistle Thrush *Turdus viscivorus* 28 cm 11 in. Found in woods, farmland, parks and gardens; also on moors in winter. Nests in trees.

Fieldfare *Turdus pilaris* 25 cm 10 in. Found in woods and, in northern Europe, in parks and gardens. Nests in trees or on buildings. In winter spreads in flocks to fields and open country with hedges and scattered trees.

Song Thrush *Turdus philomelos* 23 cm 9 in. Often seen in woods and orchards, among scattered bushes and hedges, and in parks and gardens. May be seen on lawns cocking its head to one side, as if listening but in fact looking for a worm. Drops snails on to a stone (called an anvil) to break open their shells. Nests in trees, bushes and hedges, and also on buildings.

Redwing *Turdus iliacus* 20 cm 8 in. Found in woods and, in northern Europe, in parks and gardens. In fields and open country in winter. Nests in trees and on the ground.

Song Thrush

Mistle Thrush

WHAT TO LOOK FOR

Wren Small size, upturned tail.

Dipper Dark with white breast.

Bearded Tit Tawny body with very long tail; black moustache mark (male only).

Mistle Thrush Grey-brown back, heavily spotted breast, white underwing, white on outer tail feathers.

Fieldfare Grey head and rump, chestnut back.

Song Thrush Similar to mistle thrush, but smaller size, brown back, breast more lightly spotted, buff underwing and all-brown tail.

Redwing Reddish flanks and underwing; light stripe over eye.

Fieldfare

Redwing

Ring Ouzel

male

female

male

female   Blackbird

Ring Ouzel *Turdus torquatus* 24 cm 9½ in. Lives on moors and mountain slopes, often where there are scattered trees and bushes. Nests among low plants or on rock ledges or walls.

Blackbird *Turdus merula* 25 cm 10 in. Very often seen in woods, orchards, hedges, parks and gardens; also in fields in winter. Nests in trees, bushes or hedges, on the ground or on buildings. Some blackbirds are albino birds that have white patches or may even be entirely white.

Rock Thrush *Monticola saxatilis* 19 cm 7½ in. Lives and nests on rocky ground and among trees high in mountains in western Europe, but lower down in eastern Europe.

Blue Rock Thrush *Monticola solitarius* 20 cm 8 in. Lives on rocky and stony ground from the seashore up to mountain tops. May be seen in towns in southern Europe. Nests in holes in rocks or cliffs or on buildings.

Wheatear *Oenanthe oenanthe* 15 cm 6 in. Lives in open country, from high moors and grassy hillsides down to coasts. Nests in holes in ground or in walls and rocks.

Black-eared Wheatear *Oenanthe hispanica* 14 cm 6 in. Found in rocky and sandy places, often among scattered trees and bushes. Nests in holes in walls and rocks. The male may have either a white or black throat.

Black Wheatear *Oenanthe leucura* 18 cm 7 in. Lives in rocky mountains and at sea cliffs. Nests in holes in rocks, often hiding entrance with pile of stones.

WHAT TO LOOK FOR

Ring Ouzel   Black with white breast band.

Blackbird   Male: all black with bright yellow beak. Female: dark brown all over.

Rock Thrush   Male: blue head, orange breast and tail, white band across back. Female: mottled brown with chestnut tail.

Blue Rock Thrush   Male: blue body with dark wings and tail. Female: as female rock thrush but dark brown tail.

Wheatear   Male in summer: black patch over eye with grey crown, grey back and rump. Female and male in autumn: white stripe over eye and grey-brown back with white rump.

Black-eared Wheatear   Male: black patch over eye with white to chestnut crown, buff back and white rump; black patch may extend to throat. Female: as female wheatear but dark cheek patch and darker wings.

Black Wheatear   Male: black body. Female: dark chocolate brown body. Both have white rump.

Rock Thrush

male

female

Blue Rock Thrush

male

female

Wheatear

male

female

Black-eared Wheatear

black-throated form

female

male

male

female

Ring Ouzel

male

Black Wheatear

female

Blackbird

Rock Thrush

Blue Rock Thrush

Wheatear

Black-eared Wheatear

Black Wheatear

Blackbird nestlings. The white one is an albino.

Stonechat *Saxicola torquata* 13 cm 5 in. Found on moors, on headlands at coast and on rough ground with bushes, especially gorse. Often seen perching, flicking its tail up and down. The nest is hidden in a bush or among grass.

Whinchat *Saxicola rubetra* 13 cm 5 in. Lives in similar places to stonechat, but also likes grassy areas and fields. Behaves in same way as stonechat.

Redstart *Phoenicurus phoenicurus* 14 cm 5½ in. Found in woods and among scattered trees; also in parks and gardens. Constantly flicks its tail up and down. Nests in holes in trees and walls.

Black Redstart *Phoenicurus ochruros* 14 cm 5½ in. Found on rocky ground and cliffs; also in towns, especially around factories. Constantly flicks its tail. Nests in holes in rocks and walls, and on buildings.

Nightingale *Luscinia megarhynchos* 16 cm 6½ in. Hides away among undergrowth in woods, and in thickets and hedges, sometimes around gardens. Nest concealed near ground. Very difficult to spot, but musical song can often be heard, especially at night (though other thrushes may also sing at night).

Thrush Nightingale *Luscinia luscinia* 16 cm 6½ in. Lives, nests and sings in

Stonechat
male
female
female
male
Whinchat
male
Redstart
female

WHAT TO LOOK FOR

Stonechat Male: black head (brownish in winter) with chestnut breast. Female: as male but much paler.

Whinchat Male: dark cheeks with white stripe over eye; white at base of tail. Female: as male but paler.

Redstart Male: black throat with orange breast; reddish tail. Female: buff breast and reddish tail.

Black Redstart Male: black with reddish tail. Female: as female redstart but grey-brown breast.

Nightingale Brown back and chestnut tail with plain breast.

Thrush Nightingale Grey-brown back and partly chestnut tail with lightly speckled breast.

Bluethroat Male: blue throat with red or white patch in centre. Female: dark breast band and orange patches on tail.

Robin Orange-red face and breast.

Stonechat

Whinchat

Redstart

Black Redstart

female

male

Black Redstart

Nightingale

Thrush Nightingale

the same way as nightingale. However, the two species are found together only in a narrow band across eastern Europe.

Bluethroat *Luscinia svecica* 14 cm 5½ in. Hides away among thickets and hedges, often close to water. Nest concealed near ground. There are two colour forms: the white-spotted bluethroat (*Luscinia svecica cyanecula*) of central and southern Europe, in which the blue throat patch of the male has a white centre; and the red-spotted bluethroat (*Luscinia svecica svecica*) of northern Europe, in which it has a red centre. The blue fades during the winter.

Robin *Erithacus rubecula* 14 cm 5½ in. Very often seen in woods, hedges, parks and gardens, hopping over the ground. Nests in holes in trees and walls. In Britain, robins are bold birds and often come to bird tables, but elsewhere in Europe they are shy. Robins are usually seen alone, or at most in pairs during spring and summer. They are so aggressive towards each other that they will even mistake their own reflection for another bird and attack it.

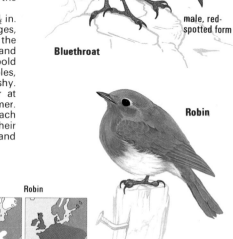

female

male, white-spotted form

male, red-spotted form

Bluethroat

Robin

Nightingale

Thrush Nightingale

Bluethroat

Robin

99

WARBLERS

Family Sylviidae

Warblers are small birds that flit about among trees, bushes and reeds, restlessly searching for insects to eat. They are named after their warbling songs, which vary widely from one species to another. The birds are often shy and difficult to spot. Most have dull colours with no very obvious marks to give away their identity. Recognizing the song of a warbler is therefore helpful in making sure of its identity.

Cetti's Warbler

Grasshopper Warbler

white form

yellow form

Savi's Warbler

Cetti's Warbler *Cettia cetti* 14 cm 5½ in. Hides away and nests among dense thickets and reed-beds beside streams and in swamps. Flicks tail.

Grasshopper Warbler *Locustella naevia* 13 cm 5 in. Hides away and nests among dense undergrowth, long grass and reeds in marshes, and in more open country with scattered trees and bushes. Named after the grasshopper-like whirring sound of its song. The underparts may be white or yellowish.

Savi's Warbler *Locustella luscinioides* 14 cm 5½ in. Lives and nests among reeds and bushes in marshes and swamps. May be seen singing while perched on the tip of a reed or top of a bush.

Moustached Warbler *Acrocephalus melanopogon* 13 cm 5 in. Lives and nests among reeds and small bushes in swamps and beside streams. Bobs its tail up and down, unlike similar sedge warbler and aquatic warbler.

Great Reed Warbler *Acrocephalus arundinaceus* 19 cm 7½ in. Found among reeds beside lakes and rivers. Builds nest around reed stems. Sings from tops of reeds and may be seen on perch in the open. Largest European warbler.

Reed Warbler *Acrocephalus scirpaceus* 13 cm 5 in. Lives and nests among reeds and low bushes beside water and sometimes in fields. Perches on reed to sing, and suspends nest among reeds.

Reed Warbler

nest in
reeds

Great Reed Warbler

Moustached Warbler

WHAT TO LOOK FOR

Cetti's Warbler Unstreaked red-brown back. Song: repeated 'chewee' in bursts.

Grasshopper Warbler Streaked back with faint eye-stripe. Song: high whirring sound held for long time.

Savi's Warbler Plumage like reed warbler but white chin. Song: like grasshopper warbler's, but lower and held for short time.

Moustached Warbler Dark streaked back; dark cap with vivid eye-stripe. Song: sweet warble with 'tu-tu-tu' sounds.

Great Reed Warbler Large; unstreaked brown back with eye-stripe. Song: loud and strident with harsh sounds.

Reed Warbler Like great reed warbler, but smaller and with faint eye-stripe. Song: monotonous mixture of sweet and harsh sounds.

Cetti's Warbler	Grasshopper Warbler	Savi's Warbler	Moustached Warbler	Great Reed Warbler	Reed Warbler

A male blackcap and young.

Aquatic Warbler

Sedge Warbler

Marsh Warbler

WHAT TO LOOK FOR

Marsh Warbler Like reed warbler, but olive-brown back and pink legs. Song: varied and musical with trills.

Sedge Warbler Like moustached warbler, but paler. Song: varied mixture of sweet and harsh sounds.

Aquatic Warbler Like sedge warbler, but buff stripe through crown. Song: like sedge warbler's.

Melodious Warbler Green-grey with yellow underside; brown legs. Song: rapid and varied, but musical.

Icterine Warbler Like melodious warbler, but blue-grey legs. Song: repeated notes, both sweet and harsh.

Olivaceous Warbler Grey-brown above and white below with buffish eye-stripe. Song: like sedge warbler's.

Blackcap Male: black cap. Female: brown cap. Song: varied warble held for short time.

Marsh
Warbler

Sedge
Warbler

Aquatic
Warbler

102

Melodious Warbler

Icterine Warbler

Olivaceous Warbler

Marsh Warbler *Acrocephalus palustris* 13 cm 5 in. Lives and nests among low bushes in thickets and swamps and beside ditches and streams; also in cornfields. Sings from low visible perch. Very like reed warbler, but unlikely to be found in reeds.

Sedge Warbler *Acrocephalus schoenobaenus* 13 cm 5 in. Lives and nests among reeds, low bushes and hedges, usually near water; also among crops. Sings from perch at top of reed, and also during short flights.

Aquatic Warbler *Acrocephalus paludicola* 13 cm 5 in. Lives and nests among reeds and low bushes beside open stretches of water. Usually shy, but may be seen and heard singing in flight.

Melodious Warbler *Hippolais polyglotta* 13 cm 5 in. Lives in woods and among bushes along rivers, also in parks and gardens. Nests in bushes and hedges. Very similar to icterine warbler in plumage, but the two species are found together only in a narrow band across the centre of Europe.

Icterine Warbler *Hippolais icterina* 13 cm 5 in. Lives and nests in same places as melodious warbler, but less likely found near water.

Olivaceous Warbler *Hippolais pallida* 13 cm 5 in. Lives and nests in trees, bushes and hedges in light woods, fields, orchards, parks and gardens. Similar to garden warbler, but the two species are usually found in different parts of Europe.

Blackcap *Sylvia atricapilla* 14 cm 5½ in. Lives and nests among undergrowth, bushes and hedges in woods, parks and gardens. Usually shy, but may come to bird tables in winter. Only the male has a black cap; the female has a brown cap.

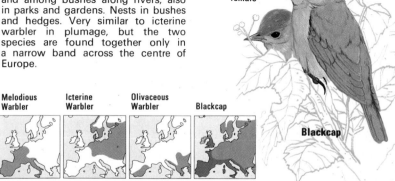

female

male

Melodious Warbler

Icterine Warbler

Olivaceous Warbler

Blackcap

Blackcap

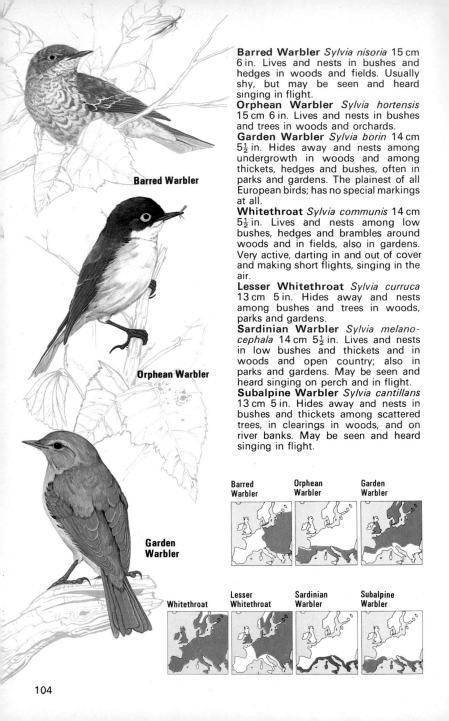

Barred Warbler *Sylvia nisoria* 15 cm 6 in. Lives and nests in bushes and hedges in woods and fields. Usually shy, but may be seen and heard singing in flight.

Orphean Warbler *Sylvia hortensis* 15 cm 6 in. Lives and nests in bushes and trees in woods and orchards.

Garden Warbler *Sylvia borin* 14 cm 5½ in. Hides away and nests among undergrowth in woods and among thickets, hedges and bushes, often in parks and gardens. The plainest of all European birds; has no special markings at all.

Whitethroat *Sylvia communis* 14 cm 5½ in. Lives and nests among low bushes, hedges and brambles around woods and in fields, also in gardens. Very active, darting in and out of cover and making short flights, singing in the air.

Lesser Whitethroat *Sylvia curruca* 13 cm 5 in. Hides away and nests among bushes and trees in woods, parks and gardens.

Sardinian Warbler *Sylvia melanocephala* 14 cm 5½ in. Lives and nests in low bushes and thickets and in woods and open country; also in parks and gardens. May be seen and heard singing on perch and in flight.

Subalpine Warbler *Sylvia cantillans* 13 cm 5 in. Hides away and nests in bushes and thickets among scattered trees, in clearings in woods, and on river banks. May be seen and heard singing in flight.

Barred Warbler

Orphean Warbler

Garden Warbler

Barred Warbler

Orphean Warbler

Garden Warbler

Whitethroat

Lesser Whitethroat

Sardinian Warbler

Subalpine Warbler

WHAT TO LOOK FOR

Barred Warbler Bars on underside. Song: musical, but in short bursts interrupted by chatter.

Orphean Warbler Black cap extending below straw-coloured eye. Song: warble of repeated phrases.

Garden Warbler Light brown above and grey-white beneath, with no obvious markings at all. Song: musical and liquid, soft but held for long time.

Whitethroat White throat with plain grey (male) or brown (female) head; red-brown wings. Song: short bursts of chatter.

Lesser Whitethroat Like whitethroat, but dark patch around eye and grey-brown wings. Song: fast rattle-like sound, often preceded by a short warble.

Sardinian Warbler Black (male) or brown (female) cap extending below red eye; grey flanks. Song: fast and musical with chattering sounds.

Subalpine Warbler Orange throat (pale in female) and white moustache. Song: slow and musical.

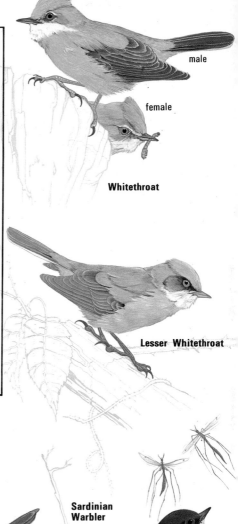

male

female

Whitethroat

Lesser Whitethroat

female

Subalpine Warbler

male

Sardinian Warbler

female

male

A pair of willow warblers at their nest in a bush. Willow warblers closely resemble chiffchaffs in appearance but their song is more musical. Willow warblers also prefer thick undergrowth whereas chiffchaffs tend to like taller trees.

Fan-tailed Warbler

female

male

Spectacled Warbler

Dartford Warbler

Spectacled Warbler *Sylvia conspicillata* 13 cm 5 in. Lives and nests in low bushes in dry open country. Sings from top of bush and in flight.

Dartford Warbler *Sylvia undata* 13 cm 5 in. Lives and nests among low bushes, especially gorse, and heather on dry open ground and hillsides. Very shy, but may sing in flight. Has generally spread its breeding range during last few years, but could be on verge of extinction in Britain, partly due to cold winters and heath fires in hot summers.

Fan–tailed Warbler *Cisticola juncidis* 10 cm 4 in. Lives and nests in dense, low plants in marshes, on lake and river banks, in fields and on plains. Often very shy, but may be seen and heard singing in flight.

Spectacled Warbler	Dartford Warbler	Fan-tailed Warbler	Willow Warbler

Willow Warbler

Chiffchaff

Wood Warbler

Bonelli's Warbler

Chiffchaff Wood Warbler Bonelli's Warbler

Willow Warbler *Phylloscopus trochilus* 11 cm 4½ in. Found scurrying and flitting about in woods, among scattered trees and bushes, and in parks and gardens. Usually nests on the ground among bushes. Virtually identical to chiffchaff, except for song.

Chiffchaff *Phylloscopus collybita* 11 cm 4½ in. Found in same places and as restless as willow warbler, but prefers areas with trees. Nests above ground. Virtually identical to willow warbler, except for song.

Wood Warbler *Phylloscopus sibilatrix* 13 cm 5 in. Lives and nests among woods and forests. Very active, singing as it moves through the leaves and flies from tree to tree.

Bonelli's Warbler *Phylloscopus bonelli* 11 cm 4½ in. Lives in woods and forests, usually on hills and mountainsides. Nests on the ground among trees.

WHAT TO LOOK FOR

Spectacled Warbler Like whitethroat, but pinker breast and darker head. Song: high, short and unvarying warble.

Dartford Warbler Red-brown breast, cocked tail. Song: short musical phrases with varying pauses.

Fan-tailed Warbler Streaked crown and back; small size with short tail. Song: repeated 'cheep cheep' sounds.

Willow Warbler Grey-green back. Yellowish underside, white eye-stripe, legs usually pale. Song: liquid warble of descending notes.

Chiffchaff Like willow warbler, but legs usually dark. Song: repeated 'chiff chaff' sounds.

Wood Warbler Yellow throat and breast, yellow eye-stripe. Song: liquid trill followed by a few long notes.

Bonelli's Warbler Like willow warbler, but greyer above, whiter beneath and with yellowish rump. Song: short trills.

GOLDCRESTS

Family Regulidae

female

male

Goldcrest

male

Firecrest

female

Goldcrests are active little birds that flit through bushes and trees, hunting for insects. In the winter, they may join flocks of tits seeking food. Two species are found in Europe, and they are the smallest European birds.

Goldcrest *Regulus regulus* 9 cm 3½ in. Found in woods and forests, especially in conifer trees; also in hedges, low bushes and undergrowth in winter. Builds basket-like nest of moss, often hung in conifer tree or among ivy.
Firecrest *Regulus ignicapillus* 9 cm 3½ in. Found in same places as gold-crest, but has no preference for conifer trees. Nest may be hung in bushes or creepers as well as in trees

Red-breasted Flycatcher

male

female

WHAT TO LOOK FOR

Goldcrest Tiny; orange (male) or yellow (female) stripe on crown.

Firecrest Like goldcrest, but black and white stripe over eye.

Spotted Flycatcher Grey-brown with lightly streaked breast and head.

Pied Flycatcher Male in summer: black back and white underside with white wing patch. Male in autumn and female: brown back with white wing patch.

Collared Flycatcher Male in summer: like pied flycatcher but white collar (western form only) and white forehead. Male in autumn and female: very like pied flycatcher.

Red-breasted Flycatcher Orange (male) or buff (female) throat; white tail edges.

Goldcrest   Firecrest   Spotted Flycatcher

Pied Flycatcher   Collared Flycatcher   Red-breasted Flycatcher

Pied Flycatcher

female (and male in autumn)

female (and male in autumn)

male (summer)

Collared Flycatcher

Spotted Flycatcher

male, western form (summer)

FLYCATCHERS

Family Muscicapidae

These birds are well named, for they are most likely to be seen sitting watchfully on a perch and then suddenly darting out to capture a fly or some other flying insect or swooping down to the ground to make a catch there. They often return to the same perch to wait for the next meal.

Spotted Flycatcher *Muscicapa striata* 14 cm 5½ in. Found at the edges of woods, among scattered trees, and in parks, orchards and gardens. Nests on buildings and tree trunks, often behind creepers. Flicks its tail as it perches. Only young birds are spotted; the adults are lightly streaked instead.

Pied Flycatcher *Ficedula hypoleuca* 13 cm 5 in. Found in woods, parks and gardens. Nests in hole in tree or wall, also in nest boxes. Flicks tail, but does not often return to same perch after chasing insects.

Collared Flycatcher *Ficedula albicollis* 13 cm 5 in. Lives in same places and behaves in same way as pied

flycatcher. In spring and summer the male's plumage varies. In Italy and central Europe, the western form (*Ficedula albicollis albicollis*), which has a white collar, is found. The eastern form (*Ficedula albicollis semitorquata*), which is found in eastern Europe, lacks the white collar.

Red–breasted Flycatcher *Ficedula parva* 11 cm 4½ in. Found in woods and parks, usually feeding among leaves in trees but sometimes chasing insects. Nests in hole in tree or wall and also on tree trunk. The male looks rather like a small robin, except that it has white on the sides of its tail.

Dunnock

Alpine Accentor

ACCENTORS

Family Prunellidae

Accentors are small birds that root about on the ground or among low plants seeking insects and spiders to eat, and also seeds in winter. Two species are found in Europe.

Dunnock or **Hedge Sparrow** *Prunella modularis* 15 cm 6 in. Found in woods, bushy countryside, hedges, parks and gardens, where it shuffles through flower beds. Resembles female house sparrow but is recognized by its narrow bill and dark grey head and underside. Nests in hedges, bushes and low plants.

Alpine Accentor *Prunella collaris* 18 cm 7 in. Lives on rocky mountain slopes, though may descend for the winter. Nests in holes in rocks.

Dunnock   Alpine Accentor   Tawny Pipit   Meadow Pipit

Tawny Pipit

A hard-working dunnock feeds a hungry young cuckoo hatched from an egg left in its nest.

Meadow Pipit

PIPITS AND WAGTAILS

Family Motacillidae

Pipits and wagtails are small birds that spend most of their time on the ground in search of insects. Pipits look like several other streaky brown ground birds, such as buntings and larks, but they can be recognized by their narrow beaks and slender bodies. Wagtails have long tails, which they wag up and down all the time.

Tawny Pipit *Anthus campestris* 16 cm 6½ in. Lives on dry, open, often sandy ground, also in fields. Nests in low plants on ground.

Meadow Pilpit *Anthus pratensis* 15 cm 6 in. Found in all kinds of open country – moors, fields, dunes, grassy slopes – and in winter in marshes and along rivers, often at the coast. Makes its nest on the ground hidden among low plants. May be seen and heard singing as it makes short flights rising from and returning to ground.

Tree Pipit *Anthus trivialis* 15 cm 6 in. Lives in light woods and clearings and among scattered trees and bushes. Nests among low plants on ground. May be seen and heard singing in short spiral flight rising from a perch.

Water Pipit *Anthus spinoletta spinoletta* 16 cm 6½ in. Lives in mountains in spring and summer, nesting in

WHAT TO LOOK FOR

Dunnock Grey head and breast with brown back.

Alpine Accentor Spotted throat and streaky flanks.

Tawny Pipit Sandy unstreaked breast and faintly streaked neck.

Meadow Pipit Pale breast with dark streaks; brown legs.

Tree Pipit Breast buff with dark streaks; pink legs.

Water Pipit Summer: unstreaked breast with grey back. Winter: like meadow pipit, but dark legs and white eye-stripe.

Rock Pipit Dark and streaky all over; dark legs; grey edges to tail (white in other pipits).

Tree Pipit   Water Pipit   Rock Pipit

holes in rock. Descends for winter, usually living near water.

Rock Pipit *Anthus spinoletta petrosus* 16 cm 6½ in. Belongs to same species as water pipit, but lives at coast, often among rocks. Nests in rock crevices.

winter

Rock Pipit

summer

Tree Pipit

Water Pipit

111

summer

winter

White Wagtail

winter

summer

Pied Wagtail

White Wagtail *Motacilla alba alba*
18 cm 7 in. Often found in open country,
usually near water, and also on farms
and in villages and towns. Nests in
holes and on ledges among rocks
and on buildings. In winter, large
groups sleep on buildings and in trees
in cities and towns.

Pied Wagtail *Motacilla alba yarrellii*
18 cm 7 in. Form of white wagtail
found mainly in British Isles. Lives and
nests in same places as the white
wagtail.

Grey Wagtail *Motacilla cinerea* 18 cm
7 in. In spring and summer, found by
streams and rivers, mostly in hills and
mountains, where it nests in hole in
wall or rock beside water. In winter,
moves to lowland rivers and lakes,
sewage farms and coast.

White Wagtail   Pied Wagtail   Grey Wagtail

female

Grey
Wagtail

male
(winter

male
(summer)

WHAT TO LOOK FOR

White Wagtail   Black and white with
very long tail; grey back.

Pied Wagtail   As white wagtail, but
black back in spring and summer.

Grey Wagtail   Grey back with yellow
underside; black throat (male in summer
only).

Yellow Wagtail   Green-brown back and
bright yellow underside (pale in female).

Yellow Wagtail Head Patterns

Blue-headed Wagtail   Blue-grey
crown, white stripe over eye, yellow
throat.

Yellow Wagtail   Olive and yellow
head.

Spanish Wagtail   Grey crown, white
stripe starting from eye, white throat.

Ashy-headed Wagtail   Grey head, no
stripe over eye, white throat.

Black-headed Wagtail   Black head,
no stripe over eye, yellow throat.

A grey wagtail feeds its young at its nest hidden in a hollow bank.

Yellow Wagtail *Motacilla flava* 16 cm 6½ in. Found in marshes and fields, usually near water. Nests on the ground, among grass or crops. Several forms with different head patterns and different names live in Europe. They all have their own regions but where these meet, intermediate forms may be seen. In southern Scandinavia and central Europe, the blue-headed wagtail (*Motacilla flava flava*) is found.

Britain is the home of the yellow wagtail (*Motacilla flava flavissima*). The Spanish wagtail (*Motacilla flava iberiae*) lives in Spain, Portugal and southern France. In Italy and Albania, the ashy-headed wagtail (*Motacilla flava cinereocapilla*) is found, and the blackheaded wagtail (*Motacilla flava feldegg*) lives in south-east Europe. Each kind may sometimes stray from its own region.

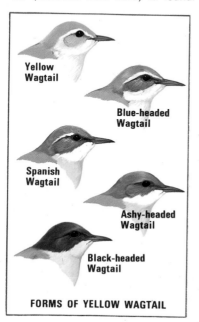

FORMS OF YELLOW WAGTAIL

Yellow Wagtail

Blue-headed Wagtail

Spanish Wagtail

Ashy-headed Wagtail

Black-headed Wagtail

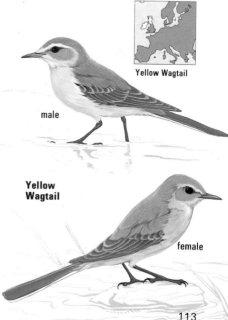

Yellow Wagtail

male

Yellow Wagtail

female

WAXWINGS
Family Bombycillidae

Waxwings are unusual birds because they do not have particular homes. Except when nesting, they continually wander in flocks from place to place, looking for fruits, berries and insects to eat. They may be seen in one place for a short time and then not again for years. Only one species is found in Europe.

Waxwing *Bombycilla garrulus* 18 cm 7 in. Found in woods, parks and gardens, busily eating berries and fruits. Nests in Arctic and spreads into Europe in winter in search of food. Every few years, too many waxwings are born and there is not enough food to go round. Great flocks then 'invade' southern and western Europe, reaching the British Isles, France, northern Italy and Yugoslavia.

SHRIKES
Family Laniidae

Shrikes are like small birds of prey. They perch in a tree or on a pole or wires or they glide or hover over a hedge, all the while keeping a sharp lookout for a likely victim. As soon as one is spotted – a juicy insect, a mouse or a small bird – the shrike darts after it and snaps it up in its hooked beak. The victim is then usually taken to the shrike's 'larder', a sharp thorn or barbed wire fence where it is impaled so that the shrike can tear it apart – a habit that has earned the shrike its other name of butcherbird.

STARLINGS

Family Sturnidae

winter

Starling

summer

summer

winter

Spotless Starling

Starlings like each other's company and live in flocks that in winter may contain thousands of birds. They wander over the ground, busily pecking here and there for food. They chatter constantly, often copying other sounds – even mechanical noises such as bells. Two species are likely to be seen in Europe.

Starling *Sturnus vulgaris* 21 cm 8½ in. Found throughout the countryside and also in towns, where flocks sleep on buildings and in trees. Nests in holes in trees or ground, on buildings and in nest boxes. As spring arrives, it loses the white spots of its winter plumage because the white tips of its feathers wear away. Also, the beak, which is dark in winter, turns yellow.

Spotless Starling *Sturnus unicolor* 21 cm 8½ in. Lives and nests in same kinds of places as starling. In spite of its name, it is slightly spotted in winter.

Great Grey Shrike *Lanius excubitor* 24 cm 9½ in. Found at edges of woods, among scattered trees and bushes and in hedges and orchards. Nests in trees and bushes.

Lesser Grey Shrike *Lanius minor* 20 cm 8 in. Found among scattered trees and bushes. Nests in trees.

Woodchat Shrike *Lanius senator* 18 cm 7 in. Found in scattered trees, bushy countryside, orchards and woods. Nests in trees.

Red-backed Shrike *Lanius collurio* 18 cm 7 in. Found in bushy places and among brambles and thickets. Nests in bushes and small trees.

WHAT TO LOOK FOR

Waxwing   Large crest; yellow tip on tail.

Great Grey Shrike   Black and white with grey back and crown.

Lesser Grey Shrike   As great grey shrike but black forehead.

Woodchat Shrike   Chestnut crown with white wing patch and rump (female paler than male).

Red-backed Shrike   Male: grey crown with chestnut back and wings. Female: plain brown back with bars on breast.

Starling   Summer: slightly-speckled glossy black with green-purple sheen. Winter: black with white spots.

Spotless Starling   Summer: as starling but unspeckled deep black. Winter: as starling but small spots.

Red-backed Shrike

Starling

Spotless Starling

female

male

Greenfinch

Hawfinch

Goldfinch

FINCHES

Family Fringillidae

Like tits, finches are generally among the most well-known and liked of birds, for they often come to gardens and parks, adding a touch of colour with their bright plumage. They are less likely to be seen in the summer when they are nesting. At other times, they may be seen, usually in groups, working their way through trees or bushes or over low plants, as they search for seeds. They have stout beaks that can split open a seed as easily as a pair of nutcrackers.

WHAT TO LOOK FOR

Hawfinch Huge beak above small black bib; wide white wingbar.

Greenfinch Green-brown with yellow edges to wings and tail (female paler than male).

Goldfinch Red patch on face; wide yellow wingbar.

Siskin Male: yellow-green with black crown and chin. Female: grey-green with streaky breast, yellow tail edges.

Linnet Male: red forehead and breast (pale in winter), grey wing patch. Female: as twite (page 118) but streaky throat and grey wing patch.

Hawfinch *Coccothraustes coccothraustes* 18 cm 7 in. Lives in woods, orchards, parks and gardens, but may hide away among leaves, especially in Britain. Nests in trees and bushes. Has huge bill that can crack open hard seeds.

Greenfinch *Carduelis chloris* 15 cm 6 in. Often seen among scattered trees and bushes, in fields, parks and gardens. Clings to net bags or wire baskets of nuts to feed, like tits. Nests in trees and bushes.

Goldfinch *Carduelis carduelis* 13 cm 5 in. Lives and nests in same places as greenfinch, but does not come to feed on nuts. Often seen climbing over thistles or on high perch. Badly named, as gold is only seen clearly on wings in flight.

A goldfinch sits quietly on its nest hidden in a raspberry bush. The characteristic yellow wingbar can only be seen clearly when the bird is in flight.

Siskin *Carduelis spinus* 12 cm 4¾ in. Found in woods, usually nesting in conifer trees and, in winter, feeding in alder and birch trees. Also seen in parks and gardens.

Linnet *Acanthis cannabina* 13 cm 5 in. Nests in low bushes, thickets and hedges, usually in open country but sometimes in parks and gardens. Roams over fields, rough pastures, and marshes in winter, sometimes in very large flocks.

Hawfinch

Greenfinch

Goldfinch

Siskin

Linnet

117

female male

Redpoll

Arctic Redpoll

female male

male and
female (winter)

Twite

female (summer)

male
(summer)

Twite *Acanthis flavirostris* 14 cm 5½ in.
Lives on moors and hills in summer,
nesting among heather and bushes and
in stone walls and rabbit burrows.
Descends for winter and roams over
open fields, marshes and seashores,
where it can often be seen in large
flocks.
Redpoll *Acanthis flammea* 13 cm 5 in.
Usually found in woods, but may be
seen in parks and gardens. Nests in
trees and bushes; often seen in alder
and birch trees in winter together with
siskins. Scandinavian redpolls are light
in colour.
Arctic Redpoll *Acanthis hornemanni*
13 cm 5 in. Nests in Arctic. Usually
seen in winter in woods, in company
with redpolls.
Serin *Serinus serinus* 11 cm 4½ in.
Found at edges of woods and in
orchards, parks and gardens. Nests in
trees and bushes.
Bullfinch *Pyrrhula pyrrhula* 15 cm
6 in. Found in woods, orchards, hedges,
parks and gardens. Nests in trees,
bushes and hedges. Raids fruit trees
for their buds.

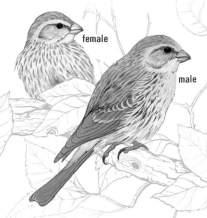

Serin

female

male

A pair of bullfinches tend their young. The bullfinch is a heavier-looking bird than most other finches and has a short sturdy bill.

male

female

Bullfinch

WHAT TO LOOK FOR

Twite Streaky brown back, head and breast, but unstreaked throat; yellow beak (winter only); pinkish rump (male).

Redpoll Red forehead and black bib; pink breast (male only).

Arctic Redpoll As redpoll but white rump.

Serin As siskin, but no yellow edges to tail and no black crown in male; also yellow rump and yellow (male) or streaky (female) forehead and breast.

Bullfinch Black crown and bright red (male) or brown-pink (female) breast.

Twite

Redpoll

Arctic Redpoll

Serin

Bullfinch

119

female

male

Pine Grosbeak

male

Crossbill

female

female

male

Parrot Crossbill

Pine Grosbeak *Pinicola enucleator*
20 cm 8 in. Lives and nests in woods,
especially among conifers and in
birch woods.
Crossbill *Loxia curvirostra* 16 cm 6½ in.
Lives and nests among conifer
(especially spruce) trees in woods and
forests. The tips of its bill are crossed
so that it can cut open fir cones to get
at the seeds. When cones are scarce,
it may spread in search of food,
reaching the British Isles, France and
Italy in great numbers.
Parrot Crossbill *Loxia pytyopsittacus*
17 cm 6¾ in. Lives and nests mainly
among pine trees, feeding in same
way as crossbill. Less likely to spread
in search of food. Gets its name from
the way it holds a cone while opening
it, rather as a parrot holds a fruit while
eating it (though crossbill performs
same action).

Pine
Grosbeak

Crossbill

Parrot
Crossbill

female

Chaffinch

male
(summer)

male
(winter)

female

male
(summer)

male
(winter)

Brambling

WHAT TO LOOK FOR

Pine Grosbeak Red (male) or green and gold (female) with two white wingbars; heavy hooked bill.

Crossbill Crossed bill (not always easy to see); orange-red (male) or green (female) with dark wings and tail.

Parrot Crossbill As crossbill but heavier bill and larger head.

Chaffinch Male: pink breast, grey-blue head (summer only) and green rump; two white wingbars and white edges to tail. Female: yellow-brown with two white wingbars and white tail edges.

Brambling Male: orange breast and base of wing; white rump; black (summer) or brown (winter) head and back. Female: as winter male but paler.

Chaffinch *Fringilla coelebs* 15 cm 6 in. Often found in woods, among scattered trees and bushes, and in fields, hedges, orchards, parks and gardens. Nests in trees and bushes; spreads to more open country in winter.

Brambling *Fringilla montifringilla* 15 cm 6 in. Nests in trees in woods, and spreads to fields, parks and gardens in winter, often with chaffinches and other finches. Found especially in beech trees.

Chaffinch   Brambling

121

Corn Bunting

BUNTINGS
Family Emberizidae

Buntings are small seed-eating birds like finches, and have similar stout bills to crack open seeds. But they are much less well-known than finches, because they do not usually come to parks and gardens and also because most of them are not brightly coloured. Buntings are most likely to be seen feeding on the ground in winter, often in groups, and also singing from a perch in spring and summer.

Several buntings, especially the females, look rather like other streaky brown ground-living birds, such as larks, pipits and sparrows. However, only buntings and sparrows have stout bills, and sparrows (page 125) have distinguishing marks that make them easy to recognize.

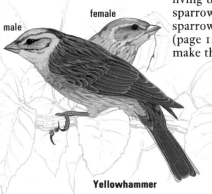

male

female

Yellowhammer

Black-headed Bunting

male

female

Corn Bunting *Emberiza calandra* 18 cm 7 in. Found in open fields and on rough ground with scattered bushes. Hides its nest in grass or low bushes. May be seen perching on a post, wall or telegraph wires.

Yellowhammer *Emberiza citrinella* 16 cm 6½ in. Found in clearings and at edges of woods, among scattered bushes, and in fields and hedges. Nests on the ground or in a low bush or hedge. Sings throughout spring and summer, repeating its famous phrase that seems to say 'little bit of bread and *no* cheese' – in fact, a group of short notes and a long one.

Black–headed Bunting *Emberiza melanocephala* 16 cm 6½ in. Lives among scattered trees and bushes; may come to gardens. Nests in low plants. Not the only bunting with a black head.

Corn Bunting

Yellowhammer

Black-headed Bunting

Cirl Bunting

Cirl Bunting
male   female

male   female

Cretzschmar's Bunting

Cirl Bunting *Emberiza cirlus* 16 cm 6½ in. Found among scattered trees and bushes and in hedges, where it nests near ground.

Cretzschmar's Bunting *Emberiza caesia* 16 cm 6½ in. Found in dry and rocky places with scattered bushes; may visit gardens. Nests on ground.

Ortolan Bunting *Emberiza hortulana* 16 cm 6½ in. Found among scattered trees and bushes, often in hills; also in fields and gardens. Nests among low plants on or near the ground.

Rock Bunting *Emberiza cia* 16 cm 6½ in. Lives in mountains on rocky slopes and among scattered trees and bushes, also in vineyards. Nests on the ground or in a low bush.

female   male

Ortolan Bunting

male   female

Rock Bunting

Cretzschmar's Bunting   Ortolan Bunting   Rock Bunting

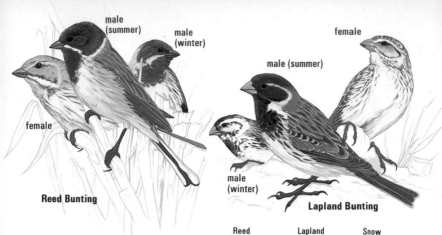

Reed Bunting

Lapland Bunting

Reed
Bunting

Lapland
Bunting

Snow
Bunting

WHAT TO LOOK FOR

Reed Bunting Male: black (summer) or brown (winter) head and throat with white moustache and collar. Female: streaky brown with white moustache.

Lapland Bunting Male: chestnut nape; black head and throat with buff eye-stripe (summer only). Female: as female reed bunting but chestnut nape.

Snow Bunting Large white wing patch with either white head (male in summer), or sandy head (male in winter), or grey-brown head (female).

Snow Finch White wings with black tips, grey head and dark chin (female duller than male).

House Sparrow Male: grey crown and black bib. Female: streaky back with plain light breast; dull eye-stripe.

Italian Sparrow Male: chestnut crown with black bib; no cheek spot. Female: as female house sparrow.

Spanish Sparrow Male: as male Italian sparrow but with large black breast patch. Female: as female house sparrow but streaky flanks.

Tree Sparrow Chestnut crown with black spot on cheek (both sexes).

Rock Sparrow Pale with stripes on head, spots on tail, yellow spot on breast.

Reed Bunting *Emberiza schoeniclus* 15 cm 6 in. Lives mainly in reed beds and swamps but also among bushes and hedges, where it nests on or near the ground. Spreads to fields in winter, and may come to bird tables in gardens.

Lapland Bunting *Calcarius lapponicus* 15 cm 6 in. Nests on ground in mountains and Arctic tundra. Moves to seashore and fields and moors near coast in winter.

Snow Bunting *Plectrophenax nivalis* 16 cm 6½ in. Nests in crevices in rocks, usually high up in mountains. Spreads in winter to open coasts, hills and fields. Usually seen in winter in flocks known as snowflakes, from the way the little white birds dance through the air.

Snow Bunting

SPARROWS

Family Ploceidae

No bird is better known than the house sparrow, which lives with man almost everywhere. Four other sparrows are also found in Europe and they too often seek man's company. Sparrows are small streaky brown birds with stout bills, rather like several buntings but having special marks that are easy to recognize. They are most often seen in groups moving busily over the ground, pecking here and there for seeds.

female
House Sparrow
male
Italian Sparrow (male)

Tree Sparrow

House Sparrow	Spanish Sparrow	Tree Sparrow	Snow Finch	Rock Sparrow

House Sparrow *Passer domesticus* 15 cm 6 in. Found in city centres and squares, parks and gardens, farms and fields. Nests under eaves, in holes in walls and rocks, and in nest boxes; also builds domed nest in creepers, bushes and trees. In Italy, Corsica and Crete, the Italian sparrow (*Passer domesticus italiae*) is found. It is a form of house sparrow with different head colours. It has a chestnut crown and white cheeks.

Spanish Sparrow *Passer hispaniolensis* 15 cm 6 in. Found in woods and among scattered trees and bushes. Nests in trees and bushes, often in old nests of other birds. Less common in towns than house sparrow and tree sparrow

Tree Sparrow *Passer montanus* 14 cm 5½ in. Found in woods, among scattered trees and bushes, and in fields and gardens. Nests in holes in trees. Also lives and nests in towns and villages like house sparrow, especially in southern and eastern Europe.

Snow Finch *Montifringilla nivalis* 18 cm 7 in. Lives on bare mountain slopes and summits, nesting in crevices. Spends winter lower down, often visiting huts and houses. Belongs to sparrow family, in spite of its name and bunting-like appearance.

Rock Sparrow *Petronia petronia* 14 cm 5½ in. Found in rocky and stony places; sometimes in gardens and among buildings. Nests in holes in rocks and trees.

Snow Finch

Rock Sparrow

female

male

Spanish Sparrow

Index
(English Names)

(Scientific Names)